"A USM graduate, Doug Heyes demonstrates in his miraculous story how we can use everything that happens in life for healing, well-being, and spiritual growth, as we awaken to the truth of who we are – divine beings having a human experience. His call to be of service to others underscores the power of love as a healing force."

— DR. H. RONALD HULNICK & DR. MARY HULNICK,
co-directors and founding faculty, University of Santa Monica –
Programs in Spiritual Psychology, and authors of
Loyalty To Your Soul: The Heart of Spiritual Psychology

"As more and more of us are led into the service of humanity's awakening, we're alarmed by how far we've separated from our spiritual Source, and enlivened by how powerfully we're coming back together. Among leaders in the holistic arts community, some would suggest they are pioneers in a field with few guide books to teach and share the infinite healing power that each and every one of us has inherited as a birthright. In *The Touch*, Doug Heyes bridges the gap with his own amazing story, profound demonstrations from his healing work, and a practical system for self-healing and facilitating healing in others. More than a compelling narrative, *The Touch* provides an easy-to-read, comprehend and apply, step-by-step guide to the inner work it will take to bring ourselves, each other, and this planet to health, resolution and peace."

— MICHAEL BRIAN BAKER, *The Breath Center*

"Doug Heyes' book, *The Touch*, is more than a fascinating read. It is a healing experience. Within our present-day accelerated extreme lifestyles, belief in the miraculous has become an essential ingredient in the recipe of healing self and the planet. The extraordinary stories and practices in these pages will inspire the belief while simultaneously providing tools to heal and transform any obstacle on our shared journey of vital health and evolving consciousness. We have a choice on this sacred journey and *The Touch* provides essential steps to carry us across the water."

— SEYMOUR KOBLIN, HHP – Founder,
International College of Holistic Studies, San Diego

"Some teachers lecture, others tell, but Doug Heyes shares – he shares his life, sincerity, and truth through the gift of storytelling and love. When there seems to be no hope, Doug exclaims through his words and actions, "Never give up." He offers simple explanations for complex theories, breathing, and meditating that will assist readers in living healthier, more holistic lives. The book, itself, is a healing experience."

— GRANDMASTER DON BAIRD, 2009 Masters Hall Of Fame

"Doug Heyes is a man who defies definition in a mere testimonial. His character is too rich, his compassion and understanding limitless, his love intoxicating, and his wisdom and healing power are the stuff of legend. I am graced by Spirit to have him in my life. He inspires me greatly. I trust and honor Doug's abilities by referring family members as clients, all of whom have experienced profound results from his practice. I too have experienced his healing power, and have no reservations recommending him to anyone who is ready to heal, grow and fill their tank with life-force."

— S.H.

"As a left-brain attorney, it's a little challenging for me to accurately describe Doug's amazing healing work, as it is unlike anything I have ever experienced. But having received the incredible benefit, I feel compelled to try. Doug facilitates a holistic healing and transformation, a release of energy on the physical, emotional and spiritual levels. A healing from the inside out. The benefits linger far beyond the session, as the body, mind and heart are shifted to a sweeter and stronger place that they do not soon forget."

— M.R.

"Doug works far deeper than the symptoms, allowing for healing to take place on the cellular level. From there, all things are possible."

— L.W.

"Doug's love and connection to Spirit run deep. Each session I have experienced with him has been a profound demonstration of that. I have experienced movement and shifting in my mind, body, and/or emotions each time I have had the opportunity to work with him. Doug is a beautiful conduit for Spirit's healing power."

— M.S.

THE TOUCH
Healing Miracles and Methods

Doug Heyes, M.A.

FINDHORN PRESS

The right of Doug Heyes to be identified as
the author of this work has been asserted by him in accordance
with the Copyright, Designs and Patents Act 1998.

Published in 2016 by Findhorn Press, Scotland

ISBN 978-1-84409-696-1

A CIP record for this title is available from the British Library.

Author photo on page 173 by Candice Land
Cover photo and all other photos by Ariana Brinckerhoff

Edited by Nicky Leach
Cover design by Richard Crookes
Interior design by Damian Keenan
Printed and bound in the USA

DISCLAIMER

The information in this book is given in good faith and is neither
intended to diagnose any physical or mental condition nor to serve
as a substitute for informed medical advice or care.
Please contact your health professional for medical advice and
treatment. Neither author nor publisher can be held liable by any
person for any loss or damage whatsoever which may arise from the
use of this book or any of the information therein.

Published by
Findhorn Press
117-121 High Street,
Forres IV36 1AB,
Scotland, UK

t +44 (0)1309 690582
f +44 (0)131 777 2711
e info@findhornpress.com
www.findhornpress.com

Contents

Dedication

Father, Mother, Divine Spirit
We join with you now in this moment of Perfect healing.
We ask for Perfect Healing for all who gather in your Light
That this healing shall forever be a demonstration
Of Your love, compassion and will for us
In our lives and in this world.
And that we will forever be witnesses to that
We ask that our connection be clear
And that whatever comes forward,
Is shared, transmitted or received,
Shall be in service of the highest good.
For this we give our love and thanks.
And so it is.

- for Grandmother

Foreword

There is a reason this is the most important time in human history, just as prophesized by Jewish mystics, many Native American tribes, and other indigenous shamans and people. Because at the very same time we might very well blow up the entire world with nuclear weapons, destroying everything with a nuclear winter, accidentally or otherwise, or we might annihilate all our ecosystems with human consumerism, we as a species are suffused with an extraordinary depth, range, and diversity of human emotional and psychological healing practices combined with spiritual mastery trainings not even known to past generations (the Course in Miracles, Pathwork, the Gene Keys, among hosts of others). The prophesies are very clear. We are either going to heal ourselves out of self- and life-destructive mindsets or we and much of the rest of life are going down… and as quickly and soon as many science fiction novels and movies predict.

"Except, as Doug Heyes makes clear in *The Touch,* this ain't no movie, this tension between mass healing and mass dying. It's a live show with extraordinary dimensions being transmitted through many lives, Heyes' included, with many of these dimensions embodied in Heyes' experiences and brought to life in his book.

"In fact, the core value of *The Touch* is its readability and accessibility. Without pronouncing it is doing so, it captures the profound meaning and opportunity of this time in a compelling narrative form that everyone should be able to relate to. Why? Because, like Heyes, we all live in the tension between what must die so we don't all die – meaning the old mindset of humanity – and what must come more alive in all of us.

"*The Touch's* compelling tale of one man's journey through the real world of experience and the realer world of psyche as it matriculates toward a saving-grace state of mind, is actually the journey the species has begun, for which the evidence abounds, with fingers crossed that it's not too late.

"Jewish mysticism doesn't prophesize the outcome. Prophesy ends in this epoch. It only says the race is on for which mindset will triumph, and the winner will be according to how many of us wake up to the reality that enfolded Heyes.

Jay Levin, founder, *L.A. Weekly*

Introduction

"I'm Talking to You Now"

"The Spirit is the Master, imagination the tool,
and the body the plastic material.
The power of the imagination is a great factor in medicine.
It may produce diseases in man and in animals,
and it may cure them. Ills of the body may be
cleared by physical remedies, or by the power
of the Spirit in action through the soul."
— PARACELSUS

If Spirit had called me ahead of time and said, "We're gonna give you a choice here. You can have this totally life-altering experience, where you'll have a healing so profound its message will become the central focus of your life and will require that you completely redefine yourself, or you can have a nice ski day," I would have flat-out chosen the nice ski day. I'd have figured my life was pretty good, didn't need much healing, my eyes were pretty well open; so thanks for the offer, but I'd really rather just ski.

So She took matters into Her own hands, flattened me on a mountainside, put Her finger on my chest, and said, "I'm talking to you now. Pay attention."

Since the things that happened, happened, I've been through a ground-up renovation and remodeling of my life. I've walked through the violet fire of transformation in every corner of my being. As these pages will attest, my awakening has been nothing short of a crucible. I'm asked to choose consistently in the direction of truth, authenticity, and service to my calling. This proves, at times, to be a daunting assignment. It reminds me of my premier grandmaster, Don Baird – a 10th degree black belt, an evolved sage, and a peaceful warrior, who recently shared, "Every day I awaken to another opportunity to fully honor my rank, and each night I retire with the knowledge that I have somehow fallen short." We are, as it turns out, human.

While this book draws deeply from personal experience, it is not about me; it is about all of us. Within each of us, there exists a wellspring of healing life force energy that can be expressed, channeled, transmitted, received, and directed for healing for ourselves and for others. While people vary widely in the extent to which they effectively use or work with this energy, it is equally and universally available to all of us at all times. The skill of working with it to support health and well-being – or to generally effect positive change – can be learned and developed. That's what The Touch is all about.

The study and practice of this phenomenon have been around for thousands of years, across virtually all cultural traditions and spiritual philosophies. Some of the techniques we'll talk about in this book can be traced back thousands of years. Part of the beauty of doing this work is the sense of being connected to something timeless. And yes, it takes time and devotion to develop mastery – but it can also provide immediate benefits.

When I first started using these methods, I got dramatically better right away. The first people I shared it with, long before I had any "technique," also got dramatically better right away. By its very nature, this work goes to deeper levels than just the physical symptoms, promoting alignment of all the levels of one's total being – physical, mental, emotional, psychological, spiritual, and so on – with the consciousness of universal healing.

Some things appear to clear up right away; other things take more time. It varies from person to person, case to case – which is one reason results can be difficult to quantify, particularly when these approaches are used in combination with other types of treatment. Whatever form it takes, it always seems to promote some level of positive change, both for the client and the healer. Every time I put my hands on someone or work with them from a distance, I'm getting it, too – the powerful circulation of pure life force energy, this dynamic, clear wave that cleanses, connects, balances, strengthens, protects, restores, rejuvenates. And whatever "stuff" I was carrying just washes away into the river of peace, presence, compassion, and love. It's beautiful beyond words.

Metaphysical leanings to the side, I have no "us and them" mentality when it comes to the western medical community. As a ski patroller and Emergency Medical Technician (EMT), I work within a specific scope of approved medical practice. When I show up to stabilize a fractured femur, I'm gonna go with a traction splint, not energy work. No doubt, I'm also doing energy work with my patient's pain and fear, to calm them and their family, to create the conditions for an optimal medical outcome.

When I got hurt, my own medical care was first rate. In the world of crisis intervention, I'm grateful for the skill and knowledge of the doctors. That said, there are still many ways in which the dominant western medical model leaves us cold. Our medical technology is thriving while our human technology is on life support, due in some measure to the faceless corporate specter of insurance, Big Pharma, and so-called "managed healthcare" – where the art of medicine becomes the science of numbers. Don't get me started...

But when dealing with health challenges, I still think of Western medicine as a very important tool on our belt. The Touch is designed as a complementary practice, to support and enhance the complete healing of the whole person; it is not intended to diagnose, treat, or cure any disease or medical condition. Be sure to discuss any proposed changes to your medical treatment with your doctor. If you need a doctor, go see one.

The basic methods and principles of The Touch are simple. They can be learned quickly and practiced immediately. This is in no way to suggest they are easy, or that this book is a manual for beginners. I liken the learning curve to chess: You can learn the moves in an hour, then spend a lifetime mastering the game.

This is a guide for dedicated spiritual travelers. If you've gotten this far, you already know the essence of what I'm sharing with you. You've already experienced it within yourself. You've already seen it operating in your life.

You're coming into ever deepening alignment with its presence and its power. You find yourself clearing the debris from your field. You're living, loving, working, breathing better already. You see the love and beauty and harmony in this world, even when it is obscured by hate and judgment and discord. You're learning to master your own darkness and use it as fuel to power your light. You're consciously raising your thoughts, your words, and your total vibration in alignment with what is true, what is necessary, and what is kind.

You are soul-centered. You know how to sit, how to think, and how to wait. You practice a high ethical standard and seek to maintain a regular spiritual practice (though, in your self-judgment, you still fall short). Your word means something. You are mindful and considerate of others; you have a consciousness that is geared toward reducing your environmental footprint. You are of well above-average intelligence. You have the capacity to hold two apparently opposed ideas in mind, and recognize the validity – or even the absurdity – of both of them.

You're driven by passion tempered with patience. You are developing intention, intuition, persistence, and wisdom. You know what it means to be courageous, to do the thing you're afraid of doing exactly when you're afraid of doing it. You derive satisfaction from being of service to others. You are creative, multifaceted, multitalented. You recognize your connection to something larger than yourself, to the Earth, to your human family, to Spirit, which animates and unites us all.

You are learning more and more to trust, to listen, to open yourself, to surrender to the true calling of your heart, to the guidance of The One within. You know that every element of the universe is present in you, and that you are a catalyst for its infinite combinations, a point of pure creative potential. You've had powerful spiritual demonstrations in your life, glimpses through the veil, and their underlying messages now inspire your work and practice, perhaps even illuminate a deeper meaning in your existence. You don't have the words to describe it, but you know it's there. In the words of Sir Arthur Eddington, Oxford astrophysicist, on the subject of quantum non-locality, "Something unknown is doing we don't know what."

We've been walking toward each other for a long time, through these dark and tangled woods. We long ago lost our compass, and our own sense of direction has been diverted, distracted, confused. Still, somehow we made our way. It is only by a perfect confluence of forces, a precise orchestration of synchronized timing, experiences, people, things, and events, large and small, that our paths now cross here on this wide open mesa. I've ridden myself weary to get here, and I can only imagine the troubles of your own trip. But at last, here we are. We made it. Drop your bundle, sit yourself down by the fire, have some soup, sing an old song or two. As the night wears on, I'll tell you a few tales from the trail and even reveal a few secrets – secrets not meant to be kept. I'll talk about some of the demonstrations that really opened my eyes.

Healing is not some mysterious, esoteric thing. It's as natural a part of who we are as being born, breathing, loving, dying. This book offers a system of simple, powerful techniques that you can use right away for your own healing, for your family, friends, animals, the planet. RAM Healing (Radiance Aesthesia Method healing), aka "The Touch," draws influences from Qi Gong, martial arts, yoga, breathwork, lightwork, prayer, meditation, spiritual psychology, intuitive energetics, harmonic resonance and quantum theory, as well as Eastern, Western, and sacred plant medicine. RAM also invokes the name of the perfect divine protector and defender, ideal father, husband, son, king. My personal icon is Hanuman, the fire monkey, avatar of Shiva, devoted friend, soldier, and servant of Lord Rama.

"Hanuman Chalisa"

— *HANUMAN MANTRA*

As I have walked this path for many years, a singular message has informed my search: *The power to heal is in all of us. It is a divine birthright of all human beings.*

CHAPTER 1

"Just Breathe"

The Best Father-Son Advice Ever!

"Love is anterior to life, posterior to death,
initial of creation, and the exponent of breath."
— EMILY DICKINSON

The first core practice of The Touch is Conscious Breathing. It is essential to bridging the gap between our narrow waking conscious awareness and the vast repository of our unconscious. Besides its well-documented benefits in cardiovascular function, mental acuity, and longevity, conscious breathing is a tool for accessing higher vibrational states, heightened perception, intuition, lucid dreaming, and natural knowing; it is a key practice for healing practitioners and clients. It is the simple act of bringing the breath into conscious awareness.

Conscious Breathing

There are numerous patterns of conscious breathing we can use, all of which provide different energetic adjustments. We will be going into depth on a variety of these patterns as we move forward in the book.

When I prepare for a session, or when I work with a client, I will almost always initiate a shared conscious breathing pattern. One of the most prevalent is a technique called Spinal Breathing.

Spinal Breathing

Uncross your arms and legs. Let your body relax and come into a comfortable, grounded, well supported position – whether you're sitting, reclining, lying down. Take a nice, deep cleansing breath. Go ahead, do that now. Do it three times, breathing deep, easy, clearing breaths and letting them go, even sighing them out. Relax… I'd tell you to close your eyes, but then you couldn't read. Let go of the jaw, the facial muscles, release any tension or holding in the neck, the throat, the chest, the diaphragm, the abdominals, the lower body centers. Let any tension, holding, or resistance drain downward through your body, your legs and your feet, into the Earth below.

With each breath, you're becoming more and more present. Thoughts and feelings will come and go; just let them do that.

Now, as you continue to deepen into your breathing, you focus your attention and awareness on your breath. As you inhale, bring the breath in through your nose and send it all the way down to the very base of your spine – to where your butt meets the chair. As you exhale, send the breath up your spine, and release it up and out the top of your head. You can choose to illuminate that pathway with a light as you breathe (you might as well get used to breathing light!). This light can be any color you choose. Got it?

STEP 1: Breathe in down the spine.
STEP 2: Breathe out up the spine.
STEP 3: Repeat steps 1 and 2 one million times.

Kidding. Sort of. If we count 12–20 breaths a minute, we're breathing about 20,000 times a day. We breathe a million times in seven weeks. The incalculable majority of those breaths – which connect us all to one another throughout all time and carry the very essence of life through our bodies – go by on autopilot, unnoticed, completely below our radar. Even when we choose to focus our awareness there, it gets away from us. We get distracted.

Don't shoot the messenger, but it's necessary to exercise discipline in order to maintain our attention. We're absolutely besieged by distraction, by reasons not to quiet ourselves and look within. The simplest thing becomes a painful chore.

I recently suggested this same conscious breathing technique to a client of mine who had been suffering with addiction issues and was in his post-treatment window following a powerful *ibogaine* experience.

He drew himself up, bigger than me. I saw tattoos I hadn't noticed before.

"You want me to *breathe?*" he glared, growling.

I shrugged, saying, "Unless you have a better idea."

Fortunately, my guy had a sense of humor.

I find a firm grasp of the ridiculous to be a useful card in my deck. "This is hard," you say. "It's hard just to do it, let alone do it while you're doing something else!"

It's a valid point, although this *is* about training your consciousness. This is a crucial step on our path to mastery, in the development of our imagination and concentration. We'll talk more about those later, but our intuitive healing craft soon comes to rely on our ability to concentrate on images to the exclusion of distraction.

So for now, just do it. Take a few minutes here and there throughout your day. A few minutes, a few times a day. That's it. Sit and breathe consciously. Believe me, I know how hard this is. I've been doing it for 40 years, and I'm still a beginner.

The resistance we experience to doing our inner work – the ambivalence, the procrastination, everything we make more important than our practice – is the same stuff that blocks us from our experience of wholeness, sufficiency, success, joy, abundance. Even with my own eccentric collection of resistances and reasons, I still manage to tune in to my breathing several times a day – pretty much whenever I remember to think about it, and always when preparing or working with a client.

So let's just fall into that nice, even, spinal breathing rhythm. Natural, unforced, easy. Sit back and take it easy. I want to tell you a story.

CHAPTER 2

Miracle on the Mountain

*"When I let go of what I am
I become what I might be."*

— LAO TZU

A bomb went off in my body. It was a snowy day in the mountains. Valentine's Day weekend, 2000, and Snow Summit in Big Bear, California, was rockin'! The first of several big winter storms had already come through, and more were on the way. The skiers and boarders were out in force. I was there on patrol, as I'd been every winter for seven years, as a volunteer for Big Bear Valley National Ski Patrol. I was 43, in excellent shape, with 36 years of skiing experience.

That morning, I left Bump (our patrol quarters at the top of the mountain) to head out on a hill check – just a morning detail of skiing a particular area of the mountain, looking for any issues, hazards, problems, anything we needed to fix, stuff like that. Nothing really stood out. Our crews keep that mountain in great shape, and this day was no exception.

For some reason, I'd left my helmet at Bump. This was unusual for me. I almost always wear a helmet when I'm on the mountain – or for any other activity where a helmet might be a good idea. I'm such a fan of helmets; I often say, "I put on a helmet to put on a helmet." So, here I was without my helmet. No big deal. I was just cruising around the mountain. No problem at all.

My hill check took me down a comeback trail and back into an area on our lower mountain that was closed to the public at the moment because the snow guns were blasting. Snowmaking equipment is very common in Southern California. As a patroller, I've skied around these guns many times. We typically close runs to the public when we're blowing snow, because it can be hazardous – buried equipment or hoses, variable snow conditions, bad visibility, disorienting noise.

I descended carefully through this area, and was making my final turn back onto an open run, when my skis ran across the berm of thick, wet, man-made snow below the last snow gun. It was like hitting a patch of glue. My skis stopped dead, but I kept going. My heel bindings clicked open perfectly, releasing me. I catapulted forward, a projectile, my trajectory inscribing an arc in space; the exclamation "Oh shit!" escaping my lips. I've heard these are the most common "famous last words."

The forward launching fall is one of the scariest in all momentum sports, as anyone who has ever gone over the handlebars of a bike, or dived into the shallow end of a pool, or been bottom slammed off a surf wave can attest. Having experienced the phenomenon enough in my adventures to have a frame of reference, I expected – as I flew through space – that my body would complete a perfect rotation in the air, that I would land flat on my back in the snow, get up laughing, brush myself off, and take a bow for the folks on the chairlift, while saying something witty and charming like, "Don't try this at home kids; this man's a professional."

Not the way it went this time.

Apparently I was closer to the ground than I thought, close enough so that I only completed a 180 degree rotation in the air, executing a perfect "pile driver" head first into the snow. That's when the bomb went off and blew me to bits.

It's said that in moments like these, you see your life flash in front of you. I didn't see my whole story, but I'm sure it was in there somewhere. I did see the flash. I was vaguely aware of motion as my body tumbled downhill like a rag doll shot from a cannon. I felt myself come apart. Whatever usually holds body and soul together had been destroyed, and pieces of me were now being scattered all over that mountain like confetti in a windstorm. Then everything stopped. My screen went totally white. No tunnel of light, no chorus of angels singing me home – just white. It might've been seconds or lifetimes.

After a time, my eyes flickered open. I found myself lying face down in the snow, spread eagled, with my head uphill. I'd been chewing gum before the crash. The gum was still in my mouth. I moved my jaw a bit and found I could still chew. I then took quick stock of the situation. I remembered everything, knew where I was, knew I'd hit a patch of soft, wet snow. I remembered my skis stopping dead and my body flying forward. I remembered the impact, the inner explosion. I told myself I hadn't been going all that fast, that I must've hit my head and knocked myself out. All this registered in an instant.

I decided I was probably okay, and attempted to get up. Nothing happened. That's when I realized I couldn't move anything from the neck down. Same with feeling: no sensation below my neck. That's when I realized I wasn't breathing. The thought crossed my mind, *Three strikes and you're out.* My training put the pieces together: a cervical spinal cord injury at the level of the phrenic nerve, paralyzing my breathing. I couldn't move, couldn't feel, couldn't breathe, couldn't key my radio to call for help. It was all I could do to lie there, feeling my life leak out of me like air from a punctured balloon. I looked up the mountain. I was dying.

That's when I saw my father standing there. A most unusual sight, since Dad had been dead for seven years. He did not look ghostly or ethereal at all. He was wearing his old brown pants and yellow windbreaker and looked like he'd just come out for a walk. I presumed he was there to take me over to the other side.

I mouthed the words, "What do I do now?" I meant, how do I complete this journey? How do I leave this broken body and join my dad higher on the mountain?

My dad spoke, giving me some of the best advice I've ever gotten.

"Just breathe."

And so I did. I glanced down again, gratefully realizing that my chest was starting to rise and fall again. Sweet, cold air filled my lungs; warm vapor puffed out. I looked up to thank my dad, but he was gone.

I still couldn't move or feel anything, but at least I was breathing again, which – let me tell you – is a definite improvement over not breathing. I started to hear radio traffic about me. One of my patrol brothers was out free skiing and had spotted my incident from the chairlift and reported it. The troops were on their way.

Let me try to put what happened next in context. We have about 150 ski patrollers associated with our resort. On any given weekend, there might be 30 of us on the hill. Of the 30 or so working that weekend, six patrollers in particular showed up to handle my incident. A random act of fate? I think not.

The first two guys to come to my rescue, Josh and Scott, were both paramedics, both devout Christian men. They started asking me the usual questions to establish my level of consciousness: Did I know where I was, the day of the week, the time of day, the name of the President?

I just looked up at them and said: "Guys, I know the answers to all of those questions. My head is fine. I can't move or feel anything from the neck down. I don't know if I'll ever be able to move or feel anything again. I think I've broken my neck and possibly severed my spinal cord. We're into some really bad shit here."

I could tell by the looks on their faces that they concurred with my assessment. Now the rest of the team showed up with the equipment: backboard, rigid C-collar, oxygen, rescue toboggan. These other four guys – Eddie, Chuck, Alex, and Rick – were top drawer patrollers, best of the best, also devoted Christian men. Eddie was a minister; Alex and Chuck were deacons in the same church.

I don't identify as a member of any particular religion. My own spiritual background could be described as eclectic. I grew up in a metaphysical tradition, in Christian Science and Religious Science. My grandmother used to take my brother and me to Christian Science Sunday school every week when we were kids. I think it was mostly to get the kids out of the house so my parents could have some alone time.

As I grew up, I explored a number of spiritual avenues – Western, Eastern, and in between, ecstatic dancing to holy rolling to meditation to mushrooms. I have always felt a powerful connection to the Divine in my life, though I've never really attributed my personal spiritual experience to lessons learned within the walls of a particular church. I've had no sense of exclusivity about my approach to worship, no "one true path," no position justifying my way or invalidating the ways of others. I have, for most of my life, referred to myself as a man of all faiths. I've always been drawn to devotional practice but never to organized religion. That said, it feels important and truthful to acknowledge that all six of the men who came to my rescue that day were Christian men, deeply involved with their faith.

The sky was dark and clouded and the snow was starting to fall harder as the boys went into the drill to get me stabilized for the trip down the mountain. We reached the point in the scenario where it was time to logroll me over on to the backboard. I looked up at the ring of concerned faces around me and knew I was in good hands. At the same moment, I saw the clouds part overhead. A bright shaft of sunlight broke through and illuminated the scene.

Then the boys went "off book" and did something that is not in our patrol manuals anywhere. (I know, I went back and checked several editions.) With a nod from Eddie, the minister, they put their hands on me and prayed. They prayed that God would be present with us at the scene, that I would be healed, and that my healing would be a demonstration of God's love, compassion, and will for me in my life and in this world, and that I would forever be a witness to that.

As they were praying, all fear left me. At once, I felt completely serene and at peace. I knew something extraordinary was happening, something much larger than I was, something in which I was only playing a part. I still had no movement or sensation, and I believed this might very well be permanent. Still, in that moment, I experienced a deep sense of surrender to the will of the Divine. Whatever my part in this cosmic drama was supposed to be, I was willing to play it – even though I had no idea what it was or what lay in store for me.

The prayer ended. The clouds once again closed overhead, blocking out the sun. The boys went to secure my hands across my chest for the toboggan ride down to the ambulance.

When they brought my right hand in and it thumped against my chest, I said, "I feel that." Same thing on the left, "I feel that."

The sensation was very vague, very distant, as if through thick padding, but it was there. I said: "Do me a favor, guys. Knock on my boots, will you?"

They did that, and I was able to correctly identify left and right. Prior to the hands-on prayer, there was no sensation at all. Immediately after the prayer, sensation began to return.

They couldn't fly me out of there. The weather was too bad and getting worse. I lay for seven hours on a gurney at our local hospital until an ambulance could take me down the hill to Loma Linda. During those hours on the table, I started to get some gross movement in the large muscles of my legs. I was able to twitch them a little.

I got excellent care at our local hospital, and also heard the first official news about my injury. I was diagnosed with a 3-level cervical spinal cord contusion, process fractures of three vertebrae, incomplete quadriplegia, and deep cord syndrome.

The attending ER doc told me this was the worst injury he'd ever seen come off that mountain – a hell of a statement from the guy who treated most of the major injuries at Southern California's busiest resort hospital. His prognosis was guarded. It was just too early to tell. We'd have to wait and see what happened when the swelling and trauma reduced, but it was pretty much a coin flip whether or not I'd be able to walk again.   Never doubting that I was being cared for by a higher authority than our local ER doctor, I grinned. "Doc," I said, "you have no idea who you're dealing with."

It was pouring rain when I was delivered like freight to Loma Linda. The rain on my face felt amazing. I remember saying to one of the EMTs that it felt like I was being baptized. He kind of smiled, as he'd already heard about what happened on the mountain. "Brother," he said, "I think you've already been baptized."

I spent the next week at Loma Linda in the critical care unit. A parade of family, friends, and fellow patrollers came to visit me. I'd watch them come in with these looks of horror and trepidation on their faces, assuming the worst. I greeted them with a glowing smile – a combination of spiritual epiphany and morphine sulfate. I told my story again and again, about the crash, the paralysis, and about the men who had put their hands on me and prayed for my healing.

I saw the change that came over my visitors when they connected with the truth of the story and realized that I was going to be all right. For my own part, I was getting better and better every day. The spinal shock subsided. The swelling around the spinal cord began to recede. Within a few days I was able to begin physical therapy – to begin to learn to use my body again.

After about a week, the chief of neurosurgery and 15 residents surrounded my bed, staring at me like a strange lab experiment. The chief told me he'd been over my case and was recommending a 3-level cervical spinal fusion to stabilize my neck and take the pressure off my spinal cord.

I looked at him and at the eager young faces of his entourage and said: "I know you're making the right medical call here, and if our positions were reversed, I'm sure I'd be saying the same thing to you. But I gotta tell you, something truly remarkable is happening here, and I think I want to wait and see what happens with my recovery before I would consent to having my neck cut open and three of my vertebrae nailed together."

I could see the guy was offended, like I was disrespecting his medical expertise. The young doctors all looked at me like I'd just told the Oracle of Delphi to screw off. I think some of them were secretly pleased.

Later that day, I received my discharge orders. Apparently, if I wasn't going to consent to surgery, then the hospital needed my bed. They brought me a list of hospitals on a clipboard and told me to select one to which I would be transferred. I had no idea where I should go. I literally closed my eyes, spun my hand around in the air, and poked the paper. My finger landed on Daniel Freeman Memorial Hospital in Inglewood.

I had no way of knowing this, but Daniel Freeman had one of the top spinal rehab centers in the country. Another example of Spirit lighting the way. I was transported there through another howling rainstorm. Between the rain and the traffic, it took several hours to make the journey, during which time the pain meds wore off. By the time I reached Daniel Freeman, I was in a world of screaming hurt.

They gave me the best room in the house. Nurse Gina came and gave me a pain shot. A little about my pain: The crushing injury to my cervical spine made it feel as though there were railroad spikes being hammered into both of my shoulders. I was also suffering from major central neuropathic pain: my skin burning from the neck down, extreme hypersensitivity and paraesthesia – the sensation of pins-and-needles but on steroids, a feeling like my body was being consumed by fire ants. On a scale of 1 to 10, I was asked to rate my pain. I think I said it was about a 57.

I was also still very weak. They did a grip test the day after I came in. I squeezed so hard I broke a sweat. They said I registered zero pounds on my left and minus 2 pounds on my right. I'm not sure how you get a minus 2, but that's what I got.

Still, despite my condition, I felt uplifted, inspired, alive. In a day or so, they brought me a wheelchair. I found that with a great deal of effort, I could push myself around. Once I realized I could get around, it was all I wanted to do.

I made endless laps around the halls and the nurses' station. My chair had a sticky wheel on the left. It took a lot more effort to push the left side and keep it going straight. I pushed so hard, I blew out a latissimus muscle on the left side. It hurt like hell, but I was elated. It was like a sports injury, a pain I could relate to!

More than anything, I felt deep gratitude and a clear sense of connection to Divine presence. I had been "saved" on that mountain. I'd heard that word before; but for the first time, I felt like I really knew what it meant. I felt like everything I'd ever believed in my heart or held as true in my faith had come through for me.

I was getting stronger fast. I started making "rounds" in my wheelchair, visiting the other patients in the spinal unit and the stroke unit next door. I spent a lot of time listening, connecting, praying. A lot of these patients were in worse shape, medically speaking, than I was. I wanted only to connect with them, to share this little miracle of healing, to bring love, strength, and hope. As I shared my story, I saw how it touched them, connected them with their faith, how it seemed in some way to make a difference.

Soon after I arrived at the hospital, I met Pat. Pat was a 300-pound African-American Baptist woman – this amazing, glorious, Earth Mother presence. I fell in love with her immediately, and she with me. She was there for pain management, and rode around on one of those little Rascal type scooters.

I sat next to her in my wheelchair at the nurses' station and told her my story of the miracle on the mountain. She studied me with rapt attention. When the story was over, she threw her arms around me, held me close, and began to pray. I'd never felt more secure, more loved and understood, more safe and protected than I did right there in Pat's massive arms. I felt as though the Earth itself was holding me.

I was doing a lot of physical therapy, beginning to take my first steps, working harder than I had ever worked before. I kept hearing from the therapists that attitude was the most important component of recovery, and that they had never met anyone with as positive an outlook and as much determination as I had.

I tried to explain. I was now grateful for each breath. Every day I could do something I couldn't do the day before. I was being given the extraordinary opportunity to rebuild myself from the ground up. This was a rebirth, an awakening, a transformation, a renewal. My old self had died up there on that mountain, and a new self had been born, touched by grace and grateful beyond words.

"Every moment of every day is a precious gift," my friend Pat said to me. "Everything we take for granted is a precious gift, and God has given you a brand new start."

I knew she was right, because I'd been talking to God about that very subject. Oh sure, we're on speaking terms. The communication comes in many ways, of course – through people, events, apparent coincidences, feelings, thoughts, perceptions, energies, sensations, impressions, illuminations.

Sometimes, there's an inner voice. For me, this particular inner voice is always female – a beautiful, loving, infinitely compassionate and wise Divine Mother-Sister-Beloved-Friend. She knows me better than I know myself and loves me without boundaries or conditions, more than I can possibly express. I'd been talking to Her a lot recently. I'd gotten in the habit of going down to the hospital chapel and spending time praying and meditating. Her voice was real clear to me in that setting. I asked why I had been saved on that mountain. Why had I been so blessed? Why was I being given this chance to start over?

She answered without hesitation, "Because I love you so much."

CHAPTER 3

Angels in the Garden

"There is nothing outside the Self."
— DEVA ALESHA CARLANDER

It wasn't long before I found The Garden. It was like my own island of paradise in the middle of an urban ocean. A block square, surrounded by tall hedges, a carpet of well-tended grass, and home to massive, ancient banyan trees, sycamores, oaks.

One of my physical therapists took me out there the first time. There was a little hill in the middle of it, which was the first mountain I climbed on my own two legs since the fall. Standing atop that little mound for the first time, I felt like I'd conquered Everest. I learned to take one step at a time, to take "one more step each day." I started spending a lot of time out there, praying, meditating, and wheelchair dancing to *Supernatural* by Carlos Santana.

One day after a session in The Garden, I went back upstairs and rolled down the hall to the spinal wing. I slowed down on the way past Macie's room. I had never been in there. Macie's room was a little scary. It was a double room, but there was no one in the front part, and the lights in that part were always off. There was only a constant dull glow, a pool of dim light from the bedside lamp in the back of the room where Macie's bed was, with this little, dark, lonesome figure sort of shriveled up under the sheets.

Macie's room had the feeling of a place you just didn't want to go. I never saw anyone besides the nursing staff go in there, never any visitors or family. I'd asked one of our nurses, a gentle black guy named Fred, what the story was. Fred kind of sadly shook his head. It wasn't looking real good for Macie. She couldn't walk (which was true for a lot of us). She wasn't participating in her therapy (a requirement for this program). She never got out of bed – and had the bedsores to prove it. She couldn't sleep, and kept the nurses busy all night with her needs, complaints, suffering. She was at the point where the hospital was ready to transfer her out to a facility where she would inevitably die – off to God's waiting room, as we used to say.

I'm not sure what motivated me that day: compassion, curiosity, Divine direction, or some combination thereof. Whatever it was, as I headed back from The Garden, I hooked a quick left turn and wheeled into Macie's room.

There in the bed lay a tiny, fragile, sweet, great grandmotherly black woman with deep, dark eyes that fixed me with a glittering, soulful gaze. I wheeled up beside her and introduced myself.

She smiled. "Oh, I know who you are," she said. "You're the miracle boy. The one from the mountain." Apparently, my legend had preceded me to Macie's room. She beckoned to me to come closer.

I wheeled up next to her bed. I told her that I'd been out in The Garden, and that something had told me to come in and see her. We spent some time together. She told me about her life – how she used to work for 50 cents a day, how she'd always felt like white people didn't care for her, how she'd always felt like a second-class citizen, how she felt so lonely and forgotten now. She was quite moved that someone would care enough to even want to come in and talk to her.

I told her that I knew one thing for certain: that God had not forgotten her. Maybe, that's why I was here – to remind her of that. She asked me to tell her my story, so I did.

When I spoke of the men who put their hands on me and prayed for my healing that day on the mountain, she held my hands as tears started to roll down her cheeks. "They told me about you," she said. "I almost didn't believe them. But here you are. And it's true. You are a miracle."

I can honestly say that my first visit with Macie was one of the most beautiful, genuine human encounters I have ever experienced.

We talked for hours. When I finally left her room that night, Fred looked up from the nurses station, grinned at me, and said, "Goodnight, Deacon."

My friend Vicky came to see me. We sat out in The Garden. I'd known Vicky since I was a teenager. We'd been close friends for 25 years. Her boyfriend when we were kids, and later her husband, Michael, had also been one of my dearest friends for 20 years.

Michael had died five years earlier from melanoma. For want of a more eloquent description, that is one raging bitch of a disease. I watched it tear Michael apart. I watched it tear Vicky apart. I watched it tear Michael and Vicky apart. Toward the end, there was so much pain, so much anger, so much grief that it overwhelmed their timeless love. When Michael died, Vicky was broken, shattered, bereft, but also somehow relieved, grateful, graced. It was a complicated time for all of us.

So there we were in The Garden. We were sitting at one of those wooden picnic tables, the kind with attached benches, under a spreading banyan tree. I was telling her the story of the men who had laid their hands on me on the mountain. She was crying. I was crying. I told her I knew there were angels in this world, that some of them wear red jackets with white crosses on them, and that there were now at least six angels in the world that I could name.

At that moment, I had the distinct impression that someone else had joined the conversation. I knew immediately who it was. I said, "Vicky, there's one more angel, and it's Michael, and he's here."

For the next little while, I'm guessing a half hour, I had the experience of channeling a conversation between Vicky and her husband. There was no conscious intent to interpret or translate on my part. The words simply flowed through me – Michael's words, my voice. Those words are private, and only for Vicky and Michael. What's important is that they got to be together. They got to say the things they wished they'd said. They got to heal and forgive themselves and each other. They got to say, "I love you," one more time.

For my own part, I felt as though I was out of my body, free floating on a river of consciousness, unbound by physical constraints, far from the world of wheelchairs and hospitals.

By and by, Michael's presence faded away, and I came back into myself to find Vicky still sitting across from me, a kind of dazed smile on her face, little makeup runs down her cheeks. She asked me if I knew what had happened. I did, though I still didn't know what to make of it. It had felt so real and so powerful, but I had no existing context for what had just taken place. I was exhausted.

Vicky and I hugged, and she went on her way. I stayed in The Garden until after dark, when the nurses started to get worried and sent someone out to look for me, finding me asleep in my wheelchair. I allowed myself to be wheeled back up to my room. I climbed into bed and lay there in the dark.

That's when Michael came to see me again. As in The Garden, this was not a visible manifestation but clearly the same presence that had visited us outside. I asked Michael what he wanted. He told me something very specific to tell his wife. It was so specific, in fact, that I didn't call Vicky right away. My own doubts stopped me. I didn't want to diminish what had happened in The Garden, in case I was just crazy. So I held onto Michael's communication throughout the whole next day; though of course, his message echoed in my mind until I was ready to go to bed that night. The last thing I did was to pick up the phone and call Vicky.

Not really knowing where to start, I just jumped in. "Vicky," I said, "Michael came to see me again last night. He told me he wanted me to tell you something."

I heard her voice quiver a bit. "Yes? What did he say?"

Here it was. I was committed. I just came out with it. "He told me he wants you to reread the letter he wrote you when the two of you first found out that he was terminal – the one you keep in the box under the bed."

Vicky just lost it on the phone. Through wracking sobs, she confirmed the existence of that letter and said that, yes, she did keep it in a box under her bed. These were facts I hadn't known till Michael told them to me and Vicky confirmed them.

She said: "I know exactly the letter you mean. I do keep it in a box under the bed. I haven't been able to read that letter for years, but when I came home last night, after what happened in The Garden, I pulled it out and reread it for the first time in years."

We held in the silence for a time. To me, this was like the Universe saying, "Just in case you think any of this is a coincidence, pay attention." And so I did.

As I drifted off to sleep that night, I lay there in the dark – the soft sounds of the hospital outside my door, the patter of the rain on my windows, the gentle reassurance of my own breath. I thought of Michael and Vicky, of God and the angels, of the men on the mountain who had put their hands on me and prayed for my healing. I felt my whole world opening up, and my heart with it. I was being touched and loved and cared for in a way I can still barely put into words – a part of something so much greater than myself, so beautiful, so real, such a sense of connection, of purpose, of having been chosen.

The next day, the rain was gone. The sun broke through the clouds. I spent most of the day out in The Garden in prayer and meditation. An ethereal mist rose from the warm, wet grass. I sat in contemplative silence in my wheelchair. Late in the day, I held up my hands. The fading sun shone through my fingers. "If it's possible for a group of guys to lay their hands on me and transmit this healing energy," I wondered aloud, "why couldn't I do that for someone else?"

Spirit's voice was soft but clear. "What makes you think you can't?"

I looked in Her direction, wherever She was. "Oh," I said, as though it was the most obvious thing in the world.

I spun my wheelchair around, headed back up to the spinal wing. The first person I saw there was Pat. She took in the look on my face, clasped her hands and uttered softly, "Praise God."

CHAPTER 4

Macie's Miracle

"Healing is the application of Loving
to the parts inside that hurt."
— DRS. RON & MARY HULNICK,
UNIVERSITY OF SANTA MONICA

"Pat," I said, "come on. I need a witness." We wheeled into Macie's room and pulled up on either side of her bed. Macie smiled, happy for the company.

"Macie," I said, "I've been out in The Garden again, and God told me He was going to allow me to heal people by putting my hands on them."

She just looked at me, beaming. I'll never forget the look of love and soul in those ancient dark eyes. "Oh, would you put your hands on me, please?" she said.

Macie had a whole list of things she wanted me to pray for: she couldn't walk, she couldn't sleep, she had these bedsores, she didn't want to die in this place, she wanted to go home.

Before I knew it, we were rolling up her nightgown and exposing her shriveled legs. I joked, "Let's not roll it up too far; I don't want to put my hands on too much." Macie cracked up laughing. So did Pat. And so it began.

I put my hands on Macie's legs and began to pray – just as the men on the mountain had prayed for me. I prayed that God would be with us, that Macie would be healed, and that her healing would forever be a demonstration of God's love, compassion, and will for her in her life and in this world, and that she would forever be a witness to that. I just improvised from there, playing variations on that theme. I asked God to allow Macie to walk again, to heal her pain, to restore her strength, to clear up the lesions on her body, to fill her with peace and happiness.

The intention was pure and clear and only rode on the rhythm of the words. Macie closed her eyes and whispered her own prayer. For her part, Pat prayed like a professional, with exclamations of devotion, celebration, joy, and grace. There was a powerful, moving, musical energy in the room.

I'm guessing the process lasted for a half hour or so. When it was over, it was clearly over. I felt like I'd just been through a major workout. I was drained but elated, exhausted, spent.

I said, "Ladies, it's been amazing, but I gotta go to bed."

I bade Pat and Macie goodnight, wheeled myself back to my room, climbed into bed, and fell asleep immediately. I don't think I moved all night. The next thing I knew it was 8:30 in the morning, time for my first physical therapy session for the day. I wheeled into PT, worked out like an animal for half an hour, then rolled back out into the hall. The first person I saw was Pat. We circled up together, talking about the night before, just sort of debriefing from the experience we had shared.

Suddenly, we heard a happy, high pitched voice, exclaiming, "There he is!"

Pat and I both turned in the direction of the voice and stared in stunned silence. Here came Macie, walking down the hall, with her astonished physical therapist beside her.

"There he is!" she repeated. "The power of Christ has done come through Doug, and I can walk again today!"

Pat and I did a classic double take, turning our stunned looks on one another for a perfect, cinematic beat, then staring back down the hall at Macie, who was coming toward us with this beaming grin on her face, walking for the first time in months.

I stood up from my wheelchair and put out my arms. Macie walked right into them. Pat and the therapist held us in their light. Macie and I just held each other for a time.

At last, she said "Praise God."

"Praise God," I agreed.

The young therapist, Chris, just looked at me again. "What did you say?" he wanted to know. "What did you do?"

"I'm not sure," I admitted. "I put my hands on her, and we prayed."

"You don't understand," Chris went on. "This is what I live for. This is why I do this work, day in, day out. To see someone get better. To maybe help them do that. Sometimes, it feels like it's all too little too late. And then something like this happens. Makes me glad I didn't call in sick today. Whatever you did in there, keep doing it."

He smiled and shook his head, saying, "Come on, Macie. All the way to the end of the hall."

Macie took Chris's arm and showed him off to us. "Isn't he handsome?"

she laughed. "I get to take a walk with this handsome young man." And off they went.

I clasped my hands and sent a blessing. Tears of gratitude began to stream down my face. Pat reached out, wrapped her arms around me, and prayed softly. I stared after Macie and Chris.

I was stunned, speechless, rejoicing inside. It was as though someone had turned on a light and now I could see. I saw that there were no mistakes, that all of this was happening for a reason. I saw the whole story in an instant: the crash on the mountain, the appearance of my father, the men who had prayed for me, the healing I had experienced, the conversations with Michael on "the other side," the sacred moment of healing with Macie and Pat, the clear illumination of my path ahead and the call to serve others in this way.

I have a favorite expression: "When God closes a door, She opens a Universe." I knew at once that this was not about me, but about the presence and power of the Divine in all of our lives. I do not claim credit for "healing" Macie. Rather, I was called upon to facilitate a process in which her own connection to Source healed her. And the beauty of working with Source is that it is boundless, and we all have equal access to it all of the time. I often tell my clients, "Spirit does the work; we just show up for the meeting."

A ribbon on the experience with Macie, the one that started me on this journey as a channel for Spirit's healing light: On the same day I left the hospital to go home, Macie also left the hospital . . . to go home.

My own healing progressed at an extraordinary rate, mind blowing even to my doctors. A year to the day after my injury, I was back at the handles of a rescue toboggan running wrecks on the mountain. At two and a half years, I completed the LA Triathlon at the Olympic distance. I continue to take part in triathlons, century rides, and other endurance events as celebrations of recovery and as fundraising opportunities for charitable causes.

I'm just a regular guy, and not a particularly religious one, certainly not within any organized definition of the word. But I do have these experiences, which have opened my eyes and have made it impossible for me to ever fully close them again. For whatever access I've been granted to the wellspring of ancient information, I give all glory and gratitude to Spirit, and to the living angels, guides, and ancestors that surround us all the time.

We are not alone. We have never been alone. Awakening into our divine nature is the essence of our journey as "spiritual beings having a human experience." It's why we're here on this planet, in physical form, in the first place. Our challenges create pathways for us to evolve into ever more conscious expressions of who we truly are. The degree to which we actually do this is a matter of choice.

We are living in a state of infinite potential, of divine opportunity. We are exponentially more creative and powerful than we ever stop to imagine. What we do with that knowledge – what we contribute, what we co-create – is entirely up to us.

CHAPTER 5

"It's in Every One of Us"

"It's in every one of us
To be wise
Find your heart
Open up both your eyes
We can all know everything
Without ever knowing why
It's in every one of us
By and by."

— DAVID POMERANZ

The central premise of this book is that we all have equal access to the healing energy of Spirit, all the time. The degree to which we connect with it and work with it in our lives is a matter of choice and practice. Certainly there are ways to augment and enhance one's own effectiveness as a channel. Some of these methods have been around for many thousands of years. But I think it's important to note that when I started working with this stuff and seeing some of the initial, surprising results, I had no technique at all.

What I had had was a demonstration of the healing energy of Spirit. In my case, it took being thrown on my head and stopped dead in my tracks to get my attention. By the way, you don't have to do that; in fact, I suggest that you don't.

The essence of this lesson is easy, natural, uplifting, liberating. You shouldn't have to hurt yourself to get it. You'd think it would be one of the first practical skills we learn as children. It should be taught in our schools. Kids are natural healers. They are far less removed from their natural imagination and creativity than most adults. They haven't yet made all the decisions and set up the machinery that keeps so many of us convinced that "we can't."

The Touch ~ Breathing Techniques

Are you remembering to breathe? We already talked about Spinal Breathing earlier in the book. The Touch incorporates a number of breathing techniques and exercises, which open the channels for healing energy to flow. Allow your breathing to become conscious again, inhaling down the spine, exhaling up the spine and out the top of the head. You're present, with calm, relaxed awareness, deepening into this pattern right now.

These various methods and movements provide different energetic attunements, both for healing practitioners and clients. It's not my objective here to "explain" these techniques for the purpose of "understanding" them. They are experientially self-explanatory. I encourage you to practice them on your own and tune into the subtle energetic variations they provide.

We use all of these methods when working with The Touch. The decision of which method to use for which person is based entirely on which method tests strongest for the client. We'll talk more about testing later. For now, you guessed it, "Just breathe."

One-Pointed Breathing

One-Pointed breathing is the most basic of the Zen meditation techniques. It involves focusing the attention and awareness on the precise point where the breath enters and leaves the body – right at the opening of the nostrils.

As simple as it sounds, this breathing technique can be extremely challenging and activating. It is much more difficult to maintain than more dynamic patterns of breathing awareness, such as Spinal Breathing, since it provides almost no distraction for the hyperactive Western "monkey mind."

This type of breathing technique is ideal for mental clarity and focus, presence, and quieting mental chatter. That makes it especially useful for clients experiencing deficits in attention, concentration, or memory. It is particularly powerful for clearing and activating the higher chakras, specifically the sixth chakra, or the psychic-intuitive center between the brows. Attention and awareness is focused exactly at the single point where the breath enters and leaves the body, right at the nostrils.

For advanced practitioners, One-Pointed breathing functions like a light switch, rapidly immersing the spiritual traveler in the clear, present, lucid state conducive to healing work.

Forward Circle Breathing

Inhale down the front of the body and around to the base of the spine. Exhale up the spine and out the top of the head. Each breath connects with the next to form a forward-turning circle of breath with the body at its center. The circle may be illuminated with a light of a chosen color.

This form supports profound positive change, helps release resistance to moving forward, to letting go of the old self, old patterns or habits, attachments, and behaviors that no longer serve. In Eastern medicine terms, it is a masculine (yang) form of breathwork that activates courage, resilience, and perseverance. It is especially relevant when moving through periods of great challenge and growth, metamorphosis, and emergence of a newly realized expression of the Self. It is very powerful for creative expression and manifestation of intention. This pattern also requires a certain counterintuitive form of attention, which provides a beneficial distraction for an overactive mental defense system.

Reverse Circle Breathing

Inhale from the base of the spine up the front of the body to the top of the head. Exhale all the way down the spine. Each breath connects with the next one to create a reverse-turning circle of breath with the body at its center. The circle may be illuminated with a light of a chosen color.

Use this breathing technique for gentle strength, balance, grounding, and drawing Earth energy. In Eastern medicine terms, it is a feminine (yin) form of breathwork that activates acceptance, trust, love, connection to the Mother, calming excessive fear, anxiety, worry, and doubt. It is especially useful for those undergoing immediate health challenges, as healing energy is drawn directly into the Self. It is a key technique for restoration, rehabilitation, rejuvenation, and reverse aging.

Microcosmic Orbit

Inhale. Follow the breath in at the nose, over the crown, and down to the base of the spine. Exhale. Follow the breath around from the base of the spine and up the front of the body.

This is perhaps the oldest and most widely practiced of all the dynamic breath meditations – the first pattern I ever worked with therapeutically, and one I use frequently in my personal practice. Use it for clarity and illumination of thought and action, and integration of mental, physical, emotional, sexual, and spiritual levels of being. It is useful for cultivating and developing *qi* (chi), the essential animating life force that energizes all things.

This practice can be traced back literally thousands of years. It comes to me by way of the Taoist traditions of my master and teacher, Dr. Baolin Wu. The power generated and circulated through this method is the stuff of legend. It's the same stuff we use to break bricks with bare hands. It is tangible, measurable, irresistible, and limitless. There's no mistake that my Qi Gong master is a kung fu master, and my kung fu master is a Qi Gong master. The regular practice of these techniques is wholly analogous to the study of martial arts as a portal to personal mastery.

Healing is an ancient, original, internal martial art. It all begins with the breath. When working with a client, it is not unusual for me to consciously synchronize my breathing with theirs. It requires great attention and focus, and makes for a powerful and deep connection. As important a tool as it is for health, longevity, and healing, Conscious Breathing is an ancient method for awakening awareness, intuition, and insight, and for attuning the practitioner to a higher spiritual frequency. If you take nothing else from this book, take this one simple technique and use it in your life.

CHAPTER 6

Imagination and Concentration

*"Imagination is more important than knowledge.
Knowledge is limited; imagination is infinite."*
— ALBERT EINSTEIN

Or, as Western Zen master trainer Werner Erhard used to say, "A dirty mind is a joy forever." In some ways, imagination has gotten kind of a bad rap, lumped in as a kind of fluffy mental activity somewhere on the order of daydreaming or fantasizing – both also useful in their own right, though not for this discussion.

When I refer to the imagination, I am referring to that center of creative consciousness that is the portal to all ideas, to every discovery and invention. It is a part of the human being that is boundless, a property of the Authentic Self. It is the interface through which we connect with Source or the Universe, residing at the nexus of body, mind, heart, and soul. It is the channel through which we bridge the island of our consciousness with the sea of our unconscious.

Every notable creation of humankind has its origins here. It is powerful beyond measure. Science is a function of imagination rigorously applied. They are not separate systems. They do not negate one another. In the realm of health and healing, they clearly work in synergy. The more we can accept that, the more we can start to tap into the limitless potential of imagination as a tool for healing.

From master 16th century physician-alchemist Paracelsus:

"The Spirit is the Master, imagination the tool, and the body the plastic material. The power of the imagination is a great factor in medicine. It may produce diseases in man and in animals, and it may cure them. Ills of the body may be cleared by physical remedies, or by the power of the Spirit in action through the soul."

For our purposes, we're looking to develop the skills of imagination and concentration, and specifically the ability to concentrate on images at will, while remaining in a relaxed, open state.

The Touch's Conscious Breathing and Light Visualization techniques are designed to activate that state of awareness. This is part of what I call the "inner kung fu" of healing, which just takes time and practice. Said my Qi Gong master, "The secret to mastery of Qi Gong is to do it, and do it, and do it." Said my kung fu master, "You can begin to say you've mastered a particular form when you've done it ten thousand times." He wasn't kidding or exaggerating. As healing artists, the way we grow is by simply doing the work. We don't have a belt system in place yet.

There's great freedom and creativity in what we're doing. The energy of creativity and the energy of healing are so closely related as to be indistinguishable. In point of fact, my first exposure to the "grounds" of imagination and concentration came by way of my early training as an actor – under the guidance of Professor George Shdanoff, artistic director of the Moscow Art Theatre with the legendary Michael Chekhov.

Those same skills of imagination and concentration, and the ability to focus the attention on images at will to the exclusion of all distractions, were among the principal skills we used to create the inner life of a character, and thereby to evoke emotional responses in the audience. In my healing work, I find I'm working with exactly the same energies. The only perceptible difference is intent, and the range of responses expands to include the other levels of experience as well – physical, mental, psychological, and spiritual, as well as emotional.

As I began to grow in this work, it was very natural for me to accept the link between imagination and healing. In Eastern medicine, the healing of the body with the mind is a core practice, and the interaction between the body and the mind is a principal factor in treatment. Little by little, these ideas are being embraced by mainstream Western medicine.

There have been many compelling studies about the relationship between prayer and healing and between spiritual healing and medical outcomes. Yes, some of them are bogus or inconclusive; some of them are downright fraudulent. But some of them are hard to ignore.

One of my personal icons is a Texas physician named Larry Dossey, who's a totally mainstream MD, medical director of a couple of major hospitals, and one of the world's leading experts in mind-body medicine (not to mention he said some really cool things about my book). Larry has conducted extensive meta-analysis of the research in the field, and shown a statistically significant relationship between patients treated with light healing methods and recovery rates in late stage cancer.

Science is telling us that the Universe is not as we once thought it to be – that it's a place where things like intelligence and observation and the non-locality of consciousness are fundamental properties that influence the very nature of what shows up in physical reality. So, if we don't close ourselves completely to the idea, we eventually have to come to grips with the notion that there's something *more* going on than we can possibly imagine! When I got to that point, I became less interested in trying to understand it, and more interested in trying to use it.

So now, we find ourselves in a confrontation with our own internal resistance to letting go and surrendering to the presence and power of something supposedly much bigger than we are that we can't exactly see. Sounds an awful lot like faith – and I respect when people have a problem with that. Unfortunately, "faith" has gotten all tangled up with "religion," and people bring their religious issues to the question of faith. All we have to do here is to recognize that everything is composed of matter and energy, and the two are in a constant state of mutual influence.

Science now recognizes that we are all interconnected and interdependent, which is sort of a technical way of saying "we're all one." And that "one" is an emanation or expression of "The One" – or, if you will, the Unified Field, as Einstein called it; the Quantum Field, as it is called in theoretical physics; or "Rumi's Field," as I call it – ("Out beyond ideas of right-doing and wrong-doing there is a field. I'll meet you there.").

Turns out they're all pointing to the same thing, in effect: the existence of a unifying "intelligent" energy that is an elemental property of the universe, operating in a domain for which the limits of conventional physics simply do not apply. A place where the speed of light is like "snail mail" in the Age of Information; where instantaneous communication across incalculable spans of space and time is not only possible but also the absolute nature of the dimension; where the universe is one of infinite, immediate possibility and potential. Now to me, that's a lot more interesting place to live than a universe that says, "I can't, because I'm too damn small."

This work makes all of us question our very conceptions of the way things are and how they operate, but you've already demonstrated that you're willing to take a look on the other side of that curtain just by reading this book. I recommend that you take it one step further: that you simply put down your ideas about what's possible, about what can happen, about what effect the mind might have on the very organization of matter. Just leave those things at the door; you can always pick them up when you leave. Just for now, set aside your considerations, judgments, values, knowledge, philosophy, religion, whatever, and just abandon yourself to this experience and to what you might discover through it.

This is not a religious practice. It is very definitely a spiritual one. So another level of the work comes from committing to and engaging in a regular practice. If you're anything like I am, when you first look through that lens, you're apt to find all kinds of conflict, questions, doubt, uncertainty, conditioning, decisions, denial – all kinds of mental and emotional constructs and self concepts that impede the pure flow of Spirit's energy and interfere with – or keep us insulated from – our natural abilities to heal and be healed.

The good news is you don't need a lot of discipline or technique when you start doing this work. You just need to start doing it. In my case, I was fortunate. I had all my defenses knocked down at once. I had to get laid flat on a mountainside so that Spirit could get my attention. It's my suggestion that you don't need to have something that traumatic happen to you in order to get this. It's there to begin with. It's part of who you are, and all you need to do is reawaken it.

Long before I had any so-called "technique," I had these demonstrations. Despite the "inconvenience" of getting paralyzed, it was the portal through which I awakened into this whole realm of healing. And I very quickly saw this stuff work – first, when I received it, then when I gave it away, then when someone I'd given it to gave it away to someone else. That's how it is. That's how it's always been. Mine is just one voice in an ancient chorus saying: *Pay attention. Look inside. There's something amazing inside you. It's right there. It's a gift. It's been there all along. Take it. Open it. Use it.*

Another part of our work, revealed through healing work, is what I call "getting out the way." Each of us arrives at this threshold with a big backpack full of judgments, habits, behaviors, reasons, garbage, and all kinds of stuff from our lives. And so when we do this work, we learn to let go of all that stuff, turn off the interference and noise in our heads, and become present, open, trusting, receptive, and surrendered. We learn to clear ourselves and open ourselves consciously to divine presence, and to gratefully offer ourselves as conduits for Spirit's boundless healing energy – so that it can do its thing with us, and through us.

This relationship keeps us focused on clearing the debris in our own lives. Not because we have to but because we want to, because nothing feels more natural or authentic to us than being in tune with – in harmony with – the energy field of Spirit. This doesn't mean we suddenly don't have challenges or issues in our own lives. I'm far from anyone's definition of perfect, and I show no signs of becoming perfect anytime soon. If and when I do, I'll announce the time of my own transition and invite all my friends to the celebration, the climax of which will be where I leave my body in full view of the crowd, leaving only my hair, robe, and fingernails and the lingering fragrance of lotus flowers. Don't hold your breath.

More good news: you don't have to be perfect to do this work; you just have to do it. It will meet you where you are, with the whole package of conflicts and contradictions that comprise your human dilemma. It will illuminate and energize your own healing. You will experience compassion and self-compassion, forgiveness and self-forgiveness, an elevation of your personal vibratory frequency, and a deepening alignment with the powerful current of Source energy that gives life to all things.

It's important to remember that this work is being done, directed and guided by Spirit. I always get a little uncomfortable when I hear the word "healer." *I* don't do any healing; that's Spirit's job, and She does it beautifully. All we do is open ourselves and invite Her to come in. As I frequently tell my clients, "When Spirit calls, pick up the damn phone!"

CHAPTER 7

Imagination to Reality

*"When we first start doing this work,
we do a lot to achieve minimal results.
As we progress, we do less and less
to achieve more and more.
Finally, when we become masters,
we achieve our most extraordinary results
by doing nothing at all."*

— DR. KAM YUEN

For the next several months following my awakening, I became a laboratory of one. I was getting stronger daily. Each day, I would greet the day with the attitude that here was another opportunity to get better. After a while, though, I hit a plateau. After such a dramatic initial recovery, things started to slow down. I was still in mind-numbing pain, so I sought the expertise and intervention of medical doctors.

I did everything imaginable that was covered by insurance. I saw neurologists, chiropractors, pain specialists, prolotherapists, physical therapists, psychotherapists, acupuncturists, you name it. I took prescription drugs, supplements, natural remedies, herbal preparations. I listened to endless well-intended counsel from well-meaning friends. It got so that I didn't want to hear it anymore. I withdrew from people so that I wouldn't have to talk about it, so that I wouldn't have to answer that pathetic "How *are* you?" I had doctors – even ones I respected – shrug and tell me to get used to it, that this kind of pain just doesn't go away.

One of the flowery floats on my hit parade was a so-called leading pain specialist. First I had to wait to be "approved" for treatment by this guy. He had to go over my case and make sure I was someone he could help. I was delighted just to get the call that he would see me. But it would take six weeks to get in to see him. Six weeks. I didn't know if I could stand it for another six minutes.

Somehow, I endured the wait, and showed up at UCLA at the appointed time for my consultation with the great doctor who was going to fix everything. They had me strip and put on a paper gown and then had me wait in a little exam room for two hours. The nurse came in with an intake form the size of a phone book. She started asking me all kinds of personal questions, way off topic for my condition. They wanted to know about my sex life, my history with drugs, whether there was any mental illness in my family, whether I'd ever suffered physical or sexual abuse, all kinds of stuff like that.

After a couple hours in a paper gown, being subjected to an interrogation, I said something like: "You know, I feel like I'm answering a lot of questions here. My appointment was for two hours ago. What do you say? Let's bring in the doc."

The nurse looked at me like I was a problem that needed solving. She extricated herself and came back a few minutes later with the doctor, a fleshy guy with no hair who smelled like cigarettes. Apparently, the nurse had reported that I was becoming "agitated." The doc was there to "handle" the patient in room 5.

He ignored the thick sheaf of notes the nurse was carrying. He started to ask me questions, which made it clear he had absolutely no idea about my case. The whole thing about getting approved for treatment, about making sure I was someone he could help? All they had done was to verify that I had insurance to cover his services.

And this guy was obviously a rock star at what he did, if the six-week waiting list was any indication. His specialty was the surgical implantation of "pain pumps" – devices that delivered pre-measured doses of morphine directly to the spinal cord. These devices were operated by a thing that looked like a garage door opener, which I would carry around with me for the rest of my life, and that needed to be routinely serviced and refilled with morphine, effectively making the patient dependent on the doctor forever. "The pain meds you're taking are candy," intoned the great doctor. "I have nuclear bombs."

I looked at this guy and said, "I've been making such great progress. I was hoping you might be able to help me in a way that's not quite so invasive."

The doctor showed no kindness or compassion. He wasn't used to being questioned. "Maybe I know more about this than you do," he pronounced.

For a guy who had stared down the chief of neurosurgery and 15 residents at Loma Linda, saying 'no' to this vampire was a walk in the park. I yanked on my pants, tore off the paper gown, headed for the door carrying my shoes. I couldn't wait to get out of there.

As I was exiting the office, the receptionist called after me. "Oh, Mr. Heyes," she said, "the doctor would like to see you again in three weeks."

"That," I replied, "will be a cold day in hell."

I was devastated. I had projected so much hope into this situation. Now, what was I going to do? Stay on pain meds forever? Take antidepressants to counteract the side effects of the pain meds? Take sleeping pills to counteract the antidepressants? Take stimulants to counteract the sleeping pills, and laxatives to counteract all that stuff? Spend my life in a brain fog, unable to work, think, write, live? This sounded a lot more like a sentence than a cure. The pain doc's heartless message echoed in my head, kept me awake at night: *Get used to it. This is your life now.* I fell into a dark place.

The phone rang. I was in no mood to answer it, but I did. It was my friend Steve, calling from New York. Steve was studying different healing methods at the time, and had come across a guy he thought I should know about. I was just about to say no, that I needed a break from doctors and therapists and practitioners, but I listened anyway.

Dr. Kam Yuen spent many years as a chiropractor and is a kung fu grandmaster. (There's that connection between healing and the martial arts again!) In fact, one of his claims to fame (or notoriety) was that he was David Carradine's martial arts master and had been technical advisor on the classic TV series, *Kung Fu*.

Dr. Yuen had developed a remarkable method for pain relief and healing and was traveling the world giving workshops on his revolutionary approach. As it happens, he was going to be in San Francisco the next weekend. Steve was already booked to attend. I figured what the hell? What do I have to lose? It'll be a nice excuse to get out of town for a few days. Maybe I'll even learn something. So I hung up from Steve, called the number he'd given me, registered for the class, and booked a room at the same hotel.

Dr. Yuen is a wise, charismatic teacher and healer, now a revered elder, still out there doing his thing – Instant Healing – traveling the world healing people and teaching people how to do it. He has the physical grace of a grandmaster, the heart of a tiger, the message of a sage, and a mind as sharp as a katana blade. By any definition, he's the real deal.

There were about 60 of us, seekers from all over the country, gathered together in a convention room at the Tiburon Lodge, across the Bay from San Francisco. We were there to learn about something called (in those days) "Chinese Energetic Medicine" and, hopefully, to be healed in the process.

I arrived with no real advance knowledge of what I was there to learn – except for my own direct experience of spiritual healing and my desire to know more about it. I can also say that while part of me really wanted to believe that this stuff was for real, I arrived with more than a little skepticism and low expectations.

On the first day, as Dr. Yuen showed us the ropes of some basic techniques, he would call participants up to the platform. One by one, they'd go up with all kinds of complaints – deep pain of one sort or another. Dr. Yuen would spend a little time with each of them, ask them some questions, get to know what he was dealing with, then he would work with them for a few minutes. He'd pinpoint underlying energetic "weaknesses" with uncanny accuracy, and "correct" them.

One by one, the participants would report a noticeable shift or change, a definite improvement in the pain or condition for which they went up on-stage. I wasn't sure what to think. Was this actually happening, or were these people "plants" in the crowd?

Then we'd do the techniques ourselves with a partner – see one, give one, get one. Within a very short time, we were all kind of amazed at what was going on. All over the room, it seemed, people were getting results. We couldn't all be plants, could we?

At the morning break, I approached Dr. Yuen and gave him a quick sketch of my story – the paralyzing injury, the amazing recovery, the overwhelming chronic pain. I told him I was taking heavy duty pain meds. I asked him if I should take them or not take them during the workshop. He looked at me for a moment – not staring into my eyes but a wider view, like he was taking in the whole picture. "Don't take them," he said. So I didn't.

As the day wore on, my pain got worse and worse, until I felt like I was going to jump out of my skin. Toward the end of the day, I raised my hand. "I believe there's something going on here," I said, "and whatever it is, I think I want it. But I gotta tell you, I feel like shit."

He glanced at me sharply and jabbed, "Maybe you need a correction between your ass and your mouth." This got a laugh from the class and from me.

Kam said, "See me right after class." I thought I was in trouble.

Class let out, and I waited in the back of the room until Dr. Yuen finished answering questions from lingering classmates. When the room cleared out, he walked back to where I was.

"Okay," he said. "Turn around, and let me take a look."

I turned around. He stood behind me, never touching me, but moving his hands over various parts of my body – my head, my neck, my back, my front. I felt my neck crack and pop, just as if I were being manually adjusted. I felt my posture shift. I felt a sensation of something moving around in my insides.

At one point, he said, "Your mother, your father, your brother, your wife, and your son," the exact distribution of my closest relatives. "Fear of not being a good provider for your family," he added, nailing one of my principal gnawing fears.

The whole session lasted about 10 minutes. When it was done, he advised me to drink plenty of fresh water and get some good rest. Then he was gone.

That's it? I thought. *Well, that was interesting.*

I was exhausted, still in pain, but I had no doubt something had just happened. I went back up to my room, downed a 1.5 liter bottle of water, watched a little mindless TV, and soon fell asleep without taking pain meds.

That night, I had two lucid dreams, which have replayed many times in similar form over the years. In the first dream, I walk into a room and find my father there. The room is familiar, though not any room I know from waking life. It just has the feeling like we've both been here before. My dad knows he's dead. I know he's dead. We both know this is a place we can come to anytime to talk about anything we want. This sequence is often a cue for lucid dreaming to me, causing me to awaken inside the dream.

The second dream is a big production number. It is also a lucid dream, perhaps by extension a part of the first, since that's how they occurred that first night in Tiburon, though they don't always play as a double feature.

In the second dream, I'm in a big, bright, urban setting – towering buildings, people in motion, cars driving by, airplanes, helicopters, a vibrating musical soundtrack. I awaken inside this dream, and I am so excited, because I know I'm dreaming and I'm in this place where it feels like I can do anything.

I'm coming up to people on the street and telling them, "Look, we're dreaming! We're all dreaming! We're all in this dream together!"

Some of the people appear not to notice me at all and just go on their way. Some kind of give me a strange look, then hurry on, like they don't really want to get involved. A few of them always come with me.

"Look," I say to them. "We can do anything we want here!" and I demonstrate by stepping out in front of an oncoming bus, facing it with a big grin on my face, spreading my arms open wide, laughing out loud as the bus passes right through me, as if matter and physics simply do not apply. I step off a building (don't ask me how I got up there) and float gently downward, touching down on the sidewalk below with effortless grace and ease. For my final trick, I teach people how to fly. We join hands, take off together, and all fly away across the bright city below.

The next morning, I awoke feeling refreshed, energized, and much better than I could remember feeling for months, and I still hadn't taken any pain meds. I reported to the class that morning that I felt like a different person.

Over the course of that first three-day experience, I did resume taking certain prescribed medications but reduced my overall intake dramatically – and did so with no ill effects or symptoms of withdrawal. My energy level increased dramatically, and my movement, strength, flexibility, and balance all improved significantly. I remember telling my classmates on the last day, "I don't know if it's possible to heal everything immediately, but I do know it's possible to get a whole lot better right away."

I remember driving back over the bridge at sunset in my rented yellow Mustang convertible – top down, music blasting, laughing out loud, belting out The Who: "I'm free… I'm free… And freedom tastes of reality… !"

I have worked with Dr. Yuen several more times over the years and think of him as one of my great master teachers. His guidance helped me to understand the human being as an energetic body whose connections extend far beyond what is physically visible, a luminous network of energy interacting in a dynamic field of energy and functioning simultaneously on multiple levels – physical, mental, emotional, spiritual, karmic, familial, ancestral, cellular, subcellular, ionic, atomic, subatomic, astrological, macrocosmic, in the memory.

The inner energy of the body continuously interacts with the outer energy of the field around it, with projections extending to the Earth, the heavens, and in all directions. Both the body and the energy field are influenced by their interaction. Expressions of symptoms are invariably connected to those deeper levels of our experience.

Western medicine, by and large, targets the physical symptoms and seeks to eliminate them by attacking them from the outside in; energy healing seeks to locate and transform the energetic weaknesses that underlie the symptoms and transform them from the inside out. Physical symptoms connect to the nonphysical levels of a person's experience, with weaknesses often occurring in the connections between principal body centers and in the interactions among those deeper levels of energy. Quantum theory demonstrates that this interaction can be influenced with the application of consciousness.

At the center of this magnificent network of human energy lies the central nervous system – the brain and spinal cord, the master computer through which all the electrochemical information travels – which innervates all the principal body systems. Through this system, we can energetically access any area of disturbance within the body, discover connections to other areas of the body, and then begin to intuitively explore the deeper levels of those connections for weaknesses and correct them. A correction in this context refers to a simple act of consciousness, like the flipping of a switch from off to on, or on to off.

In my way of working, I often use this type of scanning method as a way of locating areas of disruption or dysfunction within the energy system – we will explore these techniques shortly. I give the flipping of the switch to God. This is, in fact, the essence of The Touch. It works in sacred collaboration with Spirit. It is a devotional practice. It is a deep and timeless form of compassionate service. It is a cosmic dance, in which the boundaries of the "healer" and the "healed" are erased, as both are merged into the boundless grace and power of Spirit.

Every session I've given is also a session I've received. I'm privileged beyond words to participate with people in this way, to experience the trust, the intimacy, and the unity of a shared moment of perfect healing. It is far and away my favorite thing to do. I am humbled and grateful for the call to be of healing service.

I make it a practice to do this work whenever I am asked, without expectation of reward or compensation. I do, of course, now make my living in this field, though most of my income is from writing, teaching, and speaking. I've done many, many more sessions *pro bono* than for money. Of course, if clients can afford to pay me for my time as a professional, they are welcome to do that. Ultimately, I figure the healing is free, a gift of Spirit, just like it was for me.

When people ask me what the main thing that healed me is, I know the answer every time: "It is love," I tell them. "Without a doubt, it is love."

CHAPTER 8

"Heal This Heart" –
J . C .

"Green eyed lady, passion's lady
Dressed in love, she lives for life to be
Green eyed lady feels life I never see
Setting suns and lonely lovers free."
— JERRY CORBETTA, DAVE RIORDAN,

& J.C. PHILLIPS

This one's for my friend, J.C. Light ahead on your journey, brother. It was September 12, 2001, the day after the towers fell in New York. The world was in pain. It was the first time I remember feeling it – the pain and suffering of countless human beings. When I saw the devastation in New York, I fell to the ground, sobbing. I closed my eyes and began to pray for those who had been lost, for their families and loved ones, for the world in its time of sorrow, for all of humanity.

That's when I heard them in my meditation – uncountable voices, prayers, tears of insurmountable grief, terror, shock. I heard them, I felt them – the litany of a world in anguish. I felt as though I had tuned into God's switchboard, and all the lights were lit, all the voices merged in a mass lament.

My heart was torn open and bleeding. I wanted to help somehow, to do something, but I didn't know where to begin. So I picked up the phone. I called everyone I knew, just to check in, to see how people were doing, to try to bring some love and light, some compassion and understanding, some humanity and healing, to this unfathomable crisis.

And so it was that I called my old friend J.C.

We hadn't spoken in months. It's always astonishing how the time gets away. You just live your life, deal with the day-to-day BS, and suddenly months and years have gone by, and you've fallen out of touch with the people who have meant the most in your life. J.C. and I had been friends for nearly

30 years. We'd just fallen into the habit of not talking for months on end. I guess we just took for granted that we'd always be there, that things would be okay, that the status was forever quo. As John Lennon put it, "Life is what happens to you while you're busy making other plans."

"Hey, man," I offered. "Just callin' to check in and see how you're doin'."

"Hi, Dougie," J.C. came back. "Yeah, I'm okay."

He was lying. I knew it right away.

"What's up, man? You don't sound so good."

He brightened. "No, really, it's all right. Don't worry about me. I'm just a little freaked out, you know. Like everybody, I guess."

A confirmed showbiz guy, J.C. wasn't giving me a lot. Like me, he was a bit of a chameleon – changing the color of his skin to suit his surroundings. But my intuition was telling me something, even if J.C. wasn't. And I was beginning to trust my intuition more and more.

"Dude, what's wrong?" I pressed. "Tell me the truth." I joked a bit, "Don't make me come out there."

"No, don't. I don't want to see anybody right now."

A chill ran up my spine. I said, "That's it. I'm on my way."

J.C. became more insistent. "No. There's no reason. Don't drive all the way out here. I won't answer the door."

"Yes, you will," I assured him.

He lived about 30 miles away. I was in my car in a heartbeat, headed his way. On the way, I called our mutual friend Steve. J.C. was Steve's AA sponsor, and I figured Steve would be good emotional support. I still had no solid confirmation that there was a real problem. I was just flying on instinct. Steve and I arrived at the same time at J.C.'s eccentric ranch in the foothills to the north of the San Fernando Valley.

An eerie quiet surrounded the place. True to his word, J.C. did not answer the gate bell. Steve and I climbed over the wall and made our way past the dogs, the geese, the chickens, the exotic birds in cages. J.C.'s Jeep was in the driveway, but other than that, there was no sign of his presence.

We went around the house, knocking on doors and windows, rattling knobs, calling out for our friend. No answer.

By this time I had no doubt that something was terribly wrong. Steve and I were at the back door making all kinds of noise. Still nothing. At last we decided to break in. We were lining up for a synchronized kick to take down the back door, when we finally heard some noise from inside. We called out to J.C. Finally, he answered from inside. He sounded pissed off.

"I told you not to come out here," he growled from inside. "I told you I wouldn't answer the door."

"And here we are," I said, "and you are answering the door."

"Just go away," he said.

"That's not going to happen," I assured him. "Now you can either open the door or get out of the way, because we're coming in one way or the other."

Silence.

I looked at Steve. He shrugged. We lined up again for that kick.

"Alright, man. Stand back," I warned my friend. "We're coming in."

"Okay, okay. Wait a second," J.C. relented. We heard the click of the lock, the clatter of the latch. Finally the door opened a few inches, just to the end of the chain. J.C. peered out at us. "There. You satisfied?"

He looked bad, wearing only a ratty bathrobe, thinning hair all askew, like he'd just made his way out of bed with a bad hangover. Steve and I ruled that out quickly, as we knew our friend had been sober for over 15 years. He seemed a bit disoriented, confused, and still angry that we were there. We appealed to him in love and friendship. I told him I just wanted to check him out, to make sure he was okay. At last, he slipped the chain and opened the door.

J.C. had always been heavy, but since I'd seen him last, he had put on another 30 pounds. His skin was ashen, and a pinch of the back of his hand revealed "tenting," where the skin didn't snap back – a sign of dehydration. His pulse was equal and bilateral, and he was not complaining of any chest pain or shortness of breath. Still, he looked drawn, haggard, exhausted. I remembered that J.C. was diabetic and wondered if his condition might have been related to that.

An image of my dad flashed through my consciousness. His death eight years earlier – from what they called a "silent M.I.," a heart attack with none of the typical symptoms, had been one of the key precipitating factors in my decision to get some emergency medical training. I had always had the feeling that my dad's death could have been avoided if his condition had been recognized in time.

I had spoken to my dad by phone a couple of hours before he died. He sounded like he had a chest cold. I asked him if he had any chest pains. He actually said the words, "It feels like an elephant is sitting on my chest." I recommended that he at least call his doctor, or maybe even 911, just to rule out the possibility that he was having a heart attack. "I'm not having a heart attack," he denied. "I'm just coming down with a cold." He told me he was going to bed, to rest for a while, and that he'd be fine. That was the last conversation we ever had. I got into emergency care because I never wanted to find myself in that position again.

So here we were. I told J.C. I wanted to take him to the hospital. He refused. He said he was just hungry and tired. I told him he looked dehydrated. Finally, we made a deal: we would take him out to get something to eat and drink, then just take him over to the hospital for an exam. At last he agreed to that plan.

We got him dressed and into the car and drove to a nearby restaurant. He was hungry, ate a full lunch, and drank some water and soda. His color improved. He started to look and feel a bit better. He told us he was glad we came to check on him. It meant a lot that someone cared enough to do that.

During lunch, he told us that he'd been in a depression and had been isolating himself. He was about to turn 60 and shared with us that no male in his family had ever lived beyond that age. He was convinced that his end was near and was resigned to that fate.

After lunch he wanted to go home. He said he felt better, that he'd probably been a bit hypoglycemic, and just needed to get some food in his belly. We all wanted to believe that, but we reminded him of our deal to get checked out at the hospital. He was clearly reluctant to go. Steve had to get to a meeting and took off after lunch. I took J.C. to the hospital in my car and escorted him into the busy ER.

J.C. started to get anxious again. He clearly associated the hospital with the impending specter of death. This was the last place on Earth he wanted to be. When they put him in that stupid paper gown and wheeled him away in the chair, he looked like his life was over.

I hung out at his bedside for hours, while they wheeled him in and out and put him through a battery of tests. I don't know what tests they were running – pretty much whatever his insurance would pay for, I guess. He was dehydrated, so they gave him fluids and electrolytes. He was looking much better than he had earlier that day, though the whole hospital scene was clearly wearing on him. Finally, they informed him that all his tests looked fine and they were going to send him home. They handed him a bag with his clothes. The doctor would be down momentarily to talk to him, prior to his discharge.

He had one leg in his jeans when the doctor came in. They had just gotten the results of "the last test," and there was a dramatic change in the news.

"Mr. Phillips." The doc's words dropped like a bomb. "You're having a heart attack right now."

J.C. had one foot out the door, literally and figuratively. We stared at each other, stunned. He didn't believe it; there must be some mistake. The doctor insisted. Apparently, J.C. had a completely occluded coronary artery, and if he didn't get to the operating room right away, he was going to die. He ordered J.C. to lie back down while they got the OR ready. With paralyzing reluctance, he lay back down. The doc rushed off to do his thing.

"It's okay, man," I assured him. "God got you here in time."

"He burst into tears. "But if you hadn't shown up when you did…?"

I was quivering with emotion myself. But something moved me to take a deep breath and put my hands on his chest.

"God, we ask for perfect healing for J.C., and that this healing will forever be a demonstration of your love, compassion, and will for him in his life and in this world, and that he will forever be a witness to that." The emotion came bubbling over, as I added: "Lord, please heal this heart. Lord, please heal this heart. Lord, please heal this heart. . . !"

By now we were being swarmed with nurses and orderlies. J.C. got loaded onto a gurney and wheeled away quickly. I stood in the middle of the bustling ER, just praying after him. They let me stand there for a long time before they gently walked me out.

J.C. made a full recovery. He lived another 12 years after that – more than a decade beyond the 60-year threshold that had been the terminal station for "all the males in the Phillips family." For the rest of his life, he referred to the events of that day as "an absolute miracle."

As is often the case in situations where both spiritual and medical intercessions are applied, it is easy to rationalize, deconstruct, and invalidate the events of that day, to write them off as mere lucky coincidence. J.C. and I both believed that a Divine intelligence had perfectly orchestrated the whole dance; in this case, resulting in both spiritual rebirth and a perfect medical outcome. As I mentioned before, I have tremendous respect for the value of Western medicine. In my rescue work, I work with conventional medical methods all the time. That being said, this is the episode that made me take a look at my hands and say, "Hmmm. Maybe there really is something to all this."

As I've mentioned before, I do not take any so-called "credit" for anything that happened here; I'm merely reporting it as part of my own evolution along this path. I give all props to Spirit, and I do believe Spirit called on me to serve Her will that day and sent me a message to continue down this path.

CHAPTER 9

"Wild Horses Couldn't Drag Me Away" –
Blade

"Live as if you were to die tomorrow.
Learn as if you were to live forever."

— MAHATMA GANDHI

My own story of healing, "Miracle on the Mountain," had recently been published in *Chicken Soup for the Soul: A Book of Miracles*, and I was beginning to receive a bit of attention for my work in the healing field. A month into my masters program in Spiritual Psychology at the University of Santa Monica, I raised my hand in class and quietly shared that there was something I needed to own.

I told the class that I'd had an extraordinary experience of personal healing in my life, and that I was a healer. That I had been working for a number of years on developing and refining my approach, and if there was anyone who wanted to experience this work, I'd be happy to share it with them.

This resulted in something of a landslide of responses, and I soon found myself working week in and week out with many of my classmates, their family members, and friends. It was an extraordinary, catalytic period in my awakening into these natural gifts, which I believe are a common feature of our spiritual composition.

One of the first people to respond was a strong, outdoorsy girl named Amy, who looked like she'd stepped right off the ranch – short cropped blonde hair; sharp, aware blue eyes; blue jeans tucked into black riding boots. She came over to me on the morning break right after I'd shared.

"Ever work on a horse?" she asked pointedly.

"Not yet," I admitted, "but I'd be totally up for it." I make it a point never to refuse anyone – regardless of their species – who wants me to do this work.

"Great," she said. "What are you doing at lunch?" I had a feeling that

Whole Foods sushi wasn't the answer she was looking for.

"I think I'm, uh, going to be working on a horse?"

She grinned and quickly filled me in on the situation.

Blade was a big thoroughbred stud, the alpha male of his herd, who lived on a sprawling horse ranch up near my home in Topanga in the Santa Monica Mountains. He was getting on in horse years and had recently taken ill with a resistant infection that was defying conventional treatment. He'd lost his position of ascendancy in the herd, had been relegated to a corral by himself, and was being evaluated for possible euthanasia.

To me, Amy's cry for help was a definite last ditch effort. If we left at the start of lunch, we'd have just enough time to get up to the ranch, do a treatment, and make it back in time for class that afternoon. Without hesitation, I agreed.

It was a bright fall day, warm and sun dappled, as we drove up the long, rutted driveway under an ancient stand of California live oaks to the ranch where Blade had lived his whole life.

We were greeted by a couple of leathery ranch hands, both of whom knew Amy. They looked me up and down when she introduced me as a healer. Their skepticism was plain. "Ever been around horses before?" one of them queried, taking in my khaki Dockers and purple Calvin Klein sport shirt, sleeves rolled up to the elbows.

"I think we'll be okay," I replied neutrally.

They were concerned that Blade had been acting ornery and mean lately, obviously due to his illness. They grabbed a couple of lariats from a peg in a shed.

I shook my head. "You guys can stand by, if you want," I said, "but let's just see how this goes first. And keep those ropes out of sight."

The boys looked at each other, then back at me. "Sure," one of them said, spitting a wad of dip into the dust, "but the ranch can't take no liability if you…"

I'd stopped listening and walked past them toward the corral, where I now saw Blade. Amy followed me to the fence. I smiled and stepped through the rails. She stepped through with me into the corral.

Blade was alone, standing in the shade of a spreading oak tree, swishing his tail at the cloud of flies that besieged him. I could see that he had once been utterly magnificent: a solid 17 hands high, rich chestnut color, four white stockings, golden brown eyes that looked up at me in sadness and pain, but without a trace of "ornery" or "mean."

Doing my very best horse whisperer impression, I approached him with ease and gentleness, speaking his name in quiet reassurance, telling him I was there to help him. He nickered back softly. I had the feeling he was glad to see me. Amy stood nearby, lending her loving presence. The two ranch hands hung back by the fence, lariats in hand, waiting for Blade to turn into a three-quarter-ton wrecking machine.

As I drew close to the great old stallion, I saw the most obvious external sign of his distress: his genitals were swollen to many times their normal size, gnarled and festering, with lesions oozing yellowish pus, flies swarming all around, in a toxic feeding frenzy. It was a stomach turning sight, one that made me glad for my trauma training and calmness around body fluids.

I took a breath, continued moving toward him, keeping my gaze on his golden eyes. At last I was right beside him, inches from his left eye (the receptive side in mammals), seeing my own reflection there, as I continued to speak to him in a soft voice, telling him that he was magnificent, that I loved him, that I was there to help.

He turned his head toward me and gently nuzzled my body, as we stayed in close contact. I brought my hands up, placed them on either side of his head, and closed my eyes, allowing the barriers between us to simply dissolve. When I opened my eyes again, I could visualize him as a body of light, could feel his tremendous stature and power, could see his glorious lifetime as the crown prince of his herd, galloping like thunder through mountain meadows and meandering streams, trailing a string of fillies who only wanted to be close to him.

It was a breathtaking, emotional vision. I felt his powerful heart, his bellowing breath, his grandness, his nobility, his unbridled joy. We stayed together in that place for a long time, as my hands found different positions on his body – his head, his neck, his heart, his spine, his internal and external anatomy, circulating light through each of his centers, just as I would with a human being, only with a sense of this raw, enormous power I had never experienced before.

I returned to his head, focused again on his eyes, and did a round of an energy healing technique I call "Bright Water," sending turbulent, hydraulic waves of energy through him, cleansing, clearing, connecting, washing away the last of his inner darkness, sending it into the Earth to be used in service of growth, regeneration, and rebirth.

Finally, I just stood with him, my arms around his great neck, the side of my face pressed softly against his, in an experience of unconditional love

I sensed he both received and returned. As is often the case when I go very deep into the healing work, when the session was over, it was clearly over, as if someone had flipped a switch.

I found myself once again standing in a muddy corral amid a swarm of flies, with my arms around a big old horse. I told Blade I loved him, turned back to find Amy standing where she'd been the whole time. She wiped something from her eye.

We walked back toward the corral gate, where the ranchers were still standing by. One of them hastened to open the gate for us. As we walked out, he nodded and shook my hand.

"Thanks," he said. "I guess you *have* been around horses before."

I heard from Amy a few days later. Blade had rallied. His condition had improved markedly, and he had once again taken his lead position in the herd. Many months later, I heard that he had passed away peacefully in the shade of those same live oaks, but not before he'd enjoyed one more long run in the sun with his fillies by his side.

CHAPTER 10

On Trust and Courage –

Jenny

*"In all the great religious systems, there are divine beings
who represent the feminine face of The Divine."*
— MARIANNE WILLIAMSON

J enny is one of my angels – a soft-spoken Alabama girl by way of Aspen,
Colorado, lithe and willowy, long blonde hair and deep brown eyes to melt
the soul, a gentle but wild spirit, and deep, steely strength swathed in a sweet,
soft presence.

Jenny and I bonded during our two years together as classmates in Spiritual Psychology. Early on in the program I facilitated her through a profound
session, where she was able to process and clear a particularly traumatizing
experience from her teenage years. We have remained close friends ever since.
She was one of my first clients when I began to open up my healing practice.

During the last couple months of our second year, Jenny began to experience pain and tenderness in her pelvic area and went to the doctor for an
exam. When we spoke after her battery of tests, Jenny shared some devastat-
ing news: She had been diagnosed with an ovarian tumor, as she put it, "the
size of a baseball."

By her account, her family was in an uproar, adding great stress to the
situation. Her parents insisted on surgery, and with great misgivings, Jenny
agreed. The doctors went in and removed the tumor and began bombarding
her with drugs, adding fuel to her fears that she would never be able to bear
a child.

I was shocked when I saw her post-surgery. She was weak, sick, and pale.
The coal fire in those brown eyes had all but burned out. But the doctors were
assuring her the surgery was a success, and that she would recover. She wanted
to believe them, so as best she could, she took them at their word.

Three weeks later, she went in for a postoperative follow-up exam. To everyone's consternation, the tumor was back, as big and aggressive as ever. Her

family went into full crisis mode again, adamantly insisting that she continue with the doctors' program of more invasive surgery and more toxic drugs.

In a display of courage and divine trust that belied her weakened state (and still makes me tremble when I think about it), Jenny quietly resolved, "No, that's not how it's going to be this time."

Her family went into a tailspin, trying everything they could to push her to do it their way. But Jenny held her ground. She had already made up her mind to pursue a holistic path. She booked a three-week stay at the Optimal Health Institute, where they focus on raw foods, internal cleansing, meditation, and spiritual healing.

While Jenny was off the grid at OHI, I performed several remote sessions with her. I would sit in healing meditation, bringing Jenny into my space, visualizing her as a body of radiant light energy.

Besides the area of darkness in her second (reproductive) chakra, I was also aware of weaknesses in the energetic connections among her fourth, fifth, and sixth chakras – the heart center (Spirit), the throat (emotions and communication), and the third eye (psychic and intuitive) center. There were also numerous weaknesses throughout her endocrine, lymphatic, and cellular systems. It took several sessions to clear these apparent obstructions, but finally, when I would call Jenny into the healing light, her energy radiated with clear luminescence.

The next time I saw her was a couple of weeks later, at our six-day practicum, the culmination of our two-year masters program, held in retreat at the Hyatt Regency in Indian Wells, California. She looked better than she had the last time I saw her, but still weak and washed out, like she'd been to the wars and back.

We both threw ourselves into our practicum journey, which turned out to be one of the highest and most powerful weeks of our lives. For 15 hours a day, we did intensive processing and clearing – profound healing work. Throughout the journey, many of us went so deep into our inner work that we wound up in what we laughingly referred to as "the ICU" – laid out around the outer edges of the great hall, swaddled in blankets, lovingly attended to by the angelic assisting team.

During the last of my three visits to the ICU, I clearly had the experience of leaving my body, of floating upward above the assemblage, viewing it from on high, seeing myself lying on the floor, body shaking, eyes fluttering, mouth forming inaudible words, gracious assistants tending my Earthly vessel while I was... somewhere else.

I continued spiraling upward through the roof of the building, up and up into the space above the twinkling lights glittering in the vastness of the desert, to a place of calm, quiet, peace, and light. I experienced myself being enveloped in a kind of crystalline radiance, heard the most soothing, resonant, harmonic sounds, felt as though I was being cradled in a living, formless energy that without a doubt loved me absolutely, cared for me infinitely, forgave me without question.

I felt as though I had come home at last, that I knew this place. I had been here before. I wanted nothing more than to stay, to leave my body where it was, down there in the desert, and remain here in this pure, glorious, ecstatic state.

Even as I write these words, I see how inadequate my description of the experience is. The words simply do not reach far enough. They cannot contain the indescribable richness of this dimension where I now found myself.

I was weightless in an aurora of spectral light. Celestial sound vibration traveled through me, as though simultaneously coming from within and without. It is as if the physical confines of my body had simply disappeared, and I was one with something to which I sensed I had forever been connected, something brilliant, loving, compassionate, reassuring, timeless.

I have no idea how long I was there. It could have been minutes or hours in Earth time. At some point, I felt myself falling, and I knew I was returning to my body, which still lay where I'd left it at the side of that hotel ballroom, carefully protected for my return.

At first I felt an unfathomable sadness. As I came into waking consciousness in the room, I noticed that tears were streaming down my face. I knew that I would never forget the indescribable beauty of what I had just experienced. Somehow, the absurdity of being human struck me, and I began to shake with laughter. It seemed the most hysterically funny proposition I'd ever been presented. Human? In a body? Really? You have got to be kidding.

One of the assistants came over and asked me if I needed anything. "Water," I said, still trying to make sense of where I was – or what I was.

She poured me a cup of fresh water and supported me as I brought it to my lips and drank. The cool rush grounded me immediately. I looked around, taking in the pulsating energy of the practicum. I nodded, thanked the assistant, and sat up with my back to the wall.

That's when I noticed Jenny lying nearby, her eyes closed, her body softly trembling. She was somewhere far away from this room of time and place. I had a feeling I knew where she was.

My legs would still not support me, so I crawled over to her on my hands and knees, found my way into a sitting, cross-legged position beside her. I took several deep, cleansing breaths and held my hands – which were now literally vibrating with energy – over her body. With all the focus and concentration I could muster, I proceeded to send the prismatic light and the harmonic resonance of that dimension I had just visited into the body, mind, heart, and soul of my beautiful friend.

I was vaguely aware that around us, the practicum went on break. Two hundred people left the room for half an hour, came back, and resumed the process. Jenny and I stayed as we were – I with my hands poised above her, sending the light; she… wherever she was.

After an indeterminate time, she returned and opened her eyes. I saw a tear roll down her cheek. She smiled up at me. I smiled back at her. We stayed there for a long time, saying nothing. There were no words needed.

One of the assistants came over and asked her if she needed anything. "Water," she said. I laughed. Jenny laughed. I saw the sparkle in her eyes again.

Throughout the rest of the week, I held Jenny in my healing prayers. The practicum came to an end; we hugged each other and went back to our separate lives. A week or so later, I got the call. Jenny had been to her doctor for another exam.

"It's gone," she said. "The doctor doesn't have any explanation. The tumor is completely dissolved."

I was simply blown away. I acknowledged her for her courage, her trust, and her commitment to her relationship with Spirit.

Once again, I feel compelled to say that I take no credit for Jenny's healing. It happened as a result of her devotion to the presence and power of the Divine in her life. She took complete responsibility for her own well-being in co-creation with Spirit, determined to put herself completely into the care of The One, and a miracle happened. Our exchange was but a blip on the radar screen of universal healing consciousness – albeit one that made an unforgettable difference in both of our lives, one that validated everything both of us had ever known in our heart of hearts, one that forever changed the way we view what's possible in God's world.

POSTSCRIPT: As of this writing, Jenny is now the radiant mother of a beautiful, healthy baby girl, Gabriella!

CHAPTER 11

"Hush Little Baby" –
Sarah

*"We can easily forgive the child who is afraid of the dark;
the real tragedy of life is men who are afraid of the light."*
— PLATO

I went into retreat following my masters program in Spiritual Psychology. It was a rare opportunity to escape the demands of the world and focus on assimilating the growth I'd experienced over the past years: to pray, meditate, clear, and heal any lingering negativity, doubt, attachment, or nonserving energies. An extraordinary time of waking up and listening to the true calling of my heart.

If you ever have the opportunity to disconnect for a while from phones, computers, the media, the world, to simply follow your path of Spirit, I recommend it without reservation.

One of my retreat brothers was a former punk rocker named Jay – now a kind, easygoing traveler on the road of light – who still played a mean guitar. Like many of us on this path, Jay had been through a great deal of trauma and upheaval in his life, a lot of pain and dysfunction in his family history, and a profound journey of personal healing. It has been said that a painful youth is an advantage in the process of spiritual development.

Without going into a long list of the abuses and difficulties he had suffered, suffice it to say that Jay was a living example of this phenomenon. During the early days of our friendship, we talked a lot about things like unconditional love, healing, forgiveness (particularly self-forgiveness), about challenges as opportunities, and what it means to live in a universe of infinite possibility. At last the wounds of his wild, wild days were starting to close, and the damage between himself and his family was beginning to heal – most recently revolving around the birth of Jay's first grandchild, Sarah.

Sarah was two months old, born two months prematurely. She had spent the first six weeks of her life in a neonatal intensive care unit (NICU), being treated for a staggering list of birth issues, from low birth weight (two pounds) and susceptibility to infection to cardiac and respiratory complications due to her underdeveloped cardiopulmonary system, which featured, as Jay described it, "two big holes in her heart." The tiny infant was already making a family-sized difference, as a rallying point for three generations of loving care and the casting aside of old conflicts in favor of what was truly important.

One morning, we awoke before sunrise, as was our custom. As I pulled on white sweats for my morning devotional pilgrimage to the sacred rocks high above our camp, Jay was acting positively goofy and giddy. When I asked him what was up, he shared that he'd spoken with his daughter, Taylor, the night before. She and the rest of the family would be coming out for a visit later that day. They were bringing Sarah. It would be the first time he had seen her outside the hospital.

I told Jay I'd say a special prayer for them up in the rocks.

Dawn was absolutely breathtaking. As I went through my morning Qi Gong, an extraordinary cloud formation took the eastern sky by storm. Several of us gathered up there in those rocks, moved beyond words by what we witnessed. We all shared the same vision of the marvelous mural painted across the sky: it was Christ flying in on a great bird with wings of fire. I took it in, held it in my heart, never let it go. The image is as fresh today as it was that glorious morning.

I took the opportunity to bring Jay, Taylor, Sarah, and the rest of the family into the radiant healing light. I spent a long time up in that sacred space, breathing, chanting, praying, and meditating, repeating my mantra and affirmations. I lost count of how many times I worked through the 108 beads of my mala. When I finally opened my eyes, I was alone. Jesus-in-the-sky had long since blown away, and the lunch bell was ringing down in camp. I gathered myself up and made my way down the rugged trail to the dining hall far below.

Jay and his family were seated around the table closest to the front door when I came in. Jay pointed me out to them, and they all looked in my direction. I smiled and nodded, took a bowl of rice and a scoop of vegetables. While in retreat, I normally took my meals alone and in silence, observing the intake of food as a form of conscious sacrament. But as I passed, Jay beckoned me over and made room for me with his family. He was positively beaming with joy at being united with his loved ones.

"This is my friend Doug I was telling you about, our spiritual guru." I glanced at him, jarred by his use of that word.

"No," I said, "I'm nobody's guru. I'm just a guy."

"Right. Sorry," Jay laughed. "This is Doug, our spiritual guy."

I sat down with them, and he started making introductions – wife Teresa, daughter Taylor, son-in-law Bob, somebody's mother-in-law, somebody's niece and nephew… I greeted everyone cordially, but honestly lost the thread a bit, as my attention now focused on the tiniest member of our little party.

"And this is Sarah," said Jay. I swear his voice cracked a bit when he said her name. She was the littlest person I'd ever seen. At two months, she was still the size of a small newborn – I think they said that she was five and a half pounds. I've seen trout bigger than that. She was cradled in her mother's arms, hooked up to a portable 24-hour monitor with wires and electrodes attached to her minuscule body. She traveled at all times with a kit containing oxygen and infant CPR supplies. I beamed lovingly in her direction.

"Hi, angel," I whispered. "I've heard a lot about you."

I looked up at her mother and the others and saw that they were all looking back at me. There was something hopeful, something – expectant – in all of their eyes. I knew immediately what it was.

"Would you mind if I put my hands on her?" I asked her mother.

"Please, would you?" Taylor responded at once.

I took a breath, recalling the heavenly image I'd seen in the clouds that morning. As delicately as I have ever touched anyone, I put one hand over Sarah's heart, the other on top of her head. I brought in the column of light, circulated it through us both, closed my eyes, and prayed my healing prayer:

"Father, Mother, Divine Spirit, we join with you now in this moment of perfect healing. We ask for perfect healing for Sarah and her family, that this healing shall forever be a demonstration of your Divine love, compassion and will for them in their lives and in this world and that they will forever be witnesses to that. We ask that our connection be clear, so that whatever comes forward, is shared, transmitted, or received, shall be in service of the highest good. For this we give our love and thanks. And so it is."

I normally keep my healing prayers nondenominational, but I was sensing a particular energy and added, "In the name of Christ. Amen."

Sarah's family joined me on the "Amen." That's when I noticed gold crosses on a couple of necks around the table and was glad I'd mentioned The One who'd flown in that morning on wings of fire.

That was it. The whole session lasted less than a minute. The moment passed, and I ate my rice and veggies, chatting pleasantly with the family as though spiritual healing is just another thing you do at lunch.

I never saw Sarah again, but over the following weeks I got reports back from Jay on her progress. She was gaining weight and beginning, as Jay described it, to "thrive." Shortly, she no longer needed the monitor or the CPR kit. Within a couple months, she was up to 11 pounds and appeared as normal and healthy as any bouncing baby girl.

On the day I was getting ready to leave the retreat for my return to the "real world," Jay came to me to say goodbye. There were tears in his eyes.

"Come on, man," I joked. "You really gonna miss me that much?"

"It's Sarah," Jay said. "She went to the doctor again. You know those holes in her heart?" I nodded. "They're gone. They're healed. You did it."

I stared at him, shaking that one off, quoting one of my favorite little aphorisms: "Spirit does the work, brother. We just show up for the meeting."

Often – as this story illustrates – by the time I get there, the work is already done. Our job becomes simply to embrace what is already present. In Sarah's case, there was first rate medical care, without which it is certainly questionable whether she would have survived. But this child, in her short life, had already brought so much forgiveness to her family, so much healing, humanity, divinity – the bright center of a radiant circle of love. Her miraculous recovery is but a reflection of the miracle of her existence.

I now understood what my great teacher had taught me all those years ago: "When we first start doing this work, we *do* a lot to achieve minimal results. As we progress, we do less and less to achieve more and more. Finally, as we become masters, we achieve our most dramatic results by doing nothing at all."

God bless you, Sarah. Have an amazing life.

CHAPTER 12

Sacred Space – Prayer and Invocation

"I looked in temples, churches and mosques;
But I found the Divine within my heart."
— RUMI

Every healing opportunity is sacred. They are divine appointments, and are necessarily approached with that level of honor and respect. In the martial arts, we bow in and out of every encounter, as a way of consecrating the moment and honoring our spiritual reflection in the warrior before us. In our healing work, we show up on time, clear and prepared to work, vibrating at our highest possible harmonic frequency. We cherish and keep our clients' trust and confidentiality. I'm always moved by the degree of trust exhibited by my clients, by their willingness to walk through the dark on their way to the light. We maintain our balance and equanimity in the face of powerful physical, emotional, mental, and spiritual forces. We're sensitive to both needs and boundaries, and we take care to treat our clients with loving respect.

As healing artists, we are like spiritual athletes. Each session we facilitate is like the big game. We have to stay in training. This means we have to have a practice.

There are, of course, countless approaches to spiritual practice. I tend to incorporate what works for me and leave the rest behind. My own practice has been woven together from an amalgam of influences, from psychology to psychonautics, from endurance training to entheogenic traveling, from Ayahuasca to Zen, with roots in Eastern, Western, Native American, and South American traditions. I also bring a decidedly type-A, Western male sensibility focused on what produces results. I'm not wired to spend 20 years on a mountaintop (though in a way, as a ski patroller, I've done exactly that!).

This book offers such a practice. It combines our RAM (Radiance Aesthesia Method) Qi Gong for Practitioners – a breathing and movement form designed to activate the specific energies we work with – with the principles and methods of The Touch. We will be covering these core practices in detail shortly.

A client called me recently, obviously stressed and going though some stuff.

"Can you give me something to *do* to clear myself?" he cried. "I'm so spun out, I can barely think!"

"You know those breathing and light exercises we do?" I offered.

"Oh, yeah. Those are great!"

"Well, you know," I ventured, "you could actually *do* them."

"Oh, man," he responded without a beat, "you have no idea. Between my morning meditation and workout, my whole organic food thing, my crushing work schedule, my hot yoga, my hot girlfriend, my Chinese doctor, my American doctor, my chiropractor, my personal trainer, my guru, and my life coach – everybody's got *something* they want me to do. If I did everything they told me, I'd have no life at all. My therapist tells me I take on too much. What do you think?"

"Keep the therapist," I told him. "And maybe the hot girlfriend."

My friend's dilemma does point to a larger pattern, which operates in a lot of us on one level or another. It's this driving-force logic system deep in our programming that compels us to want to do more, that makes us believe we need to work harder on ourselves, that the solution to the riddle of our lives lies somehow around the next bend in the road, that if we stay focused and work really hard, maybe we'll find it. Someday.

Do we all see what a trap this is? If we exile our satisfaction and happiness to some distant horizon, to some point in the indeterminate future that can be reached only when some idealized definition of ourselves is magically attained, how can we ever hope to be happy or satisfied?

To suggest that everything we need, all the answers we seek, all the love and beauty and abundance, lies right here, right now, in this present moment, free of all the wounds of the past and the fears of the future – this is pure anathema to our logic system. No matter how much we want to believe it, nothing could be that simple. *Right here, right now? Ridiculous. Now can you give me something to do to fix myself that I won't have time to do, anyway, because I'm too busy doing all this other stuff to try and fix myself?*

Point taken. A compelling argument for keeping it simple. And this is not about teaching you something you don't know; it's about awakening something that has always been in you. Once familiar with The Touch, you can tune yourself for a session in about 15 minutes.

Consecrating the Space

To begin, we consecrate the space. A personal healing sanctum, of course, is ideal – a place used only for meditation, prayer, and healing, containing luminous chakra colors and subtle fragrant hints of lavender, sage, and cinnamon, and your personal sacred objects and instruments, and a healing mat or table – the tools of your trade. This, of course, is not always available; I find my work has me traveling a lot. I carry a folding chair, a massage table, and a guitar in my car.

While not specific to The Touch, music, as a healing agent, cannot be overstated. Even 4,000 years ago, Pythagoras, the original rock star, believed that music should never be used for entertainment purposes only. Music was an expression of *Harmonia,* the divine principle that brings order to chaos and discord.

Music and harmonic resonance play an important part in my private and public practice. Different modalities call for different accoutrements: singing bowls, tuning forks, gongs, flutes, chimes, drums, crystals, essential oils – all tools for opening channels to Source. Pythagoras created instruments tuned to perfect intervals and specific harmonic ratios, and he used them to perform "Soul Adjustments," during which he "aligned souls to their divine nature," and so cured diseases of the body, emotions, and spirit. In essence, he healed people with music. In the new age, a lot of us find an iPod works pretty well.

I don't carry a lot of other stuff, since I do most of my work with my hands, heart, and mind. I do like to light a candle, which represents The Light. I've worn my mala beads in virtually every healing session I've ever conducted. These were given to me by one of my most revered teachers, and have been charged over the years with hundreds of thousands of prayers, mantras, and affirmations. I have a silk prayer shawl from Tibet that gets a lot of airplay in my healing space, particularly around our medicine circles. I use it to transmute energy and send it to the Four Winds. I also have a feather (which fell from the sky and landed on my feet) tied with a Peruvian beaded leather band, studded with a crystal heart, which I use as a "talking stick"; it represents truth and clarity. These items are spiritually charged and carry authentic meaning for me. Their presence in the space helps to sanctify it, to focus our awareness in the sacred healing moment. The client may also wish to bring a special object into the space, to charge it with the energy of our healing session to use later. That's pretty much it for my little black bag.

I bow slightly and offer a silent blessing whenever I enter anyone's home, and I leave my sandals at the door. I've left many pairs of sandals at front doors around California. I carry backups in the trunk. It's convenient that I usually work barefoot.

When entering the room where the healing work is to be done, I will pause for a moment and touch the threshold. This cues me to enter the space switched on to my highest possible spiritual frequency. I need room to move around my client, who will be seated or lying down. I might clear or rearrange the space as necessary. I like to work in cozy dens, offices, studios, family rooms. Not so much bedrooms, for a lot of energetic and ethical reasons. I generally stay out of hallways, high traffic areas, or rooms full of computers or video equipment. I usually carry some colored fabric or silk to drape over the TV screen if there is one present in the room.

It's definitely good to work outside – gardens, decks, patios, gazebos, glades – weather and privacy permitting, of course. The presence of water, particularly flowing water, is a huge asset. Nothing beats doing the work out in nature – in the mountains, under the trees, beside a river, lake, or ocean. Try it with your client floating in a hot mineral spring!

Before the session, I might clear and energize the space by burning a little white sage or palo santo, a fragrant, resinous South American tree wood related to frankincense, myrrh, and copal. They are excellent for removing any stagnant energies, and their fragrances communicate directly with the higher chakras to stimulate intuition, creativity, openness, and receptivity. We should check with our clients for any possible allergies to these substances or sensitivity to smoke. A light spray of atomized solutions of essential oils such as lavender, rose, or cedar can be used for the same purpose.

We spend a little time consulting and creating a bond of trust. We'll initiate a Conscious Breathing rhythm, illuminating the breath pattern with a light of a chosen color.

Calling in the Light

Since we work a lot with light, we begin with an invocation known as "Calling In the Light," derived from our tradition in Spiritual Psychology at University of Santa Monica:

Father, Mother, Divine Spirit, Lord God of all creation, we ask just now for a clearing; that we may be filled, surrounded, and protected by the Light of the Holy Spirit, and that any doubt, fear, tension, or worry, any debris or obstruction to the free flow of Divine Source energy, any negativity of any kind that can be lifted, now be taken up into the highest realms of light and sound, there to be transmuted and used in service of regeneration and rebirth, and dispersed back into the nothingness from which it came. We open our hearts to your guidance and will for the Highest Good. And so it is.

The Healing Prayer

We then formally consecrate our gathering with prayers and invocations. The first and most frequent of these for me is a version of the Healing Prayer my brothers on the mountain prayed over me at the scene of my rescue. I use this one every time I do healing work:

Father, Mother, Divine Spirit
We join with you now in this moment of Perfect Healing
We ask for Perfect Healing for (Client's name)
That this healing shall forever be a demonstration
Of Your love, compassion, and will for her
In her life and in this world
And that she will forever be a witness to that
We ask that our connection be clear
And that whatever comes forward,
Is shared, transmitted, or received
Shall be in service of the highest good
For this we give our love and thanks
And so it is.

The Four Directions

If I am working with a larger group, I will often invoke the Four Directions, during which the group will turn and face the corresponding compass points, as:

EAST (Yellow, Wind)

Hail, Guardians of the Watchtowers of the East
Powers of Air
We invoke you and call you
Golden Eagle of the Dawn
Star-seeker, Whirlwind, Rising Sun, Come!

By the Air that is Her Breath
Send forth your Light
Be here now!

SOUTH *(Red, Fire)*

Hail Guardians of the Watchtowers of the South
Powers of Fire
We invoke you and call you
Red Lion of the noon heat
Flaming One, Summer's warmth, Spark of Life, Come!
By the Fire that is Her Spirit
Send forth your Flame
Be here now!

WEST *(Blue, Water)*

Hail, Guardians of the Watchtowers of the West
Powers of Water
We invoke you and call you
Serpent of the watery abyss
Rainmaker, Gray-robed Twilight, Evening Star, Come!
By the Waters of her Living Womb
Send forth your Flow
Be here now!

NORTH *(Black, Earth)*

Hail, Guardians of the Watchtowers of the North
Powers of Earth, Cornerstone of all Power
We invoke you and call you
Lady of the Outer Darkness
Black bull of Midnight
Center of the whirling Sky
Stone, Mountain, Fertile Field, Come!
By the Earth that is Her Body
Send forth your Strength
Be here now!

This invocation is extremely powerful and grounding in ancient Earth energy, home-grown in sacred Native American soil. It calls in the Ancients, the elementals, Heaven and Earth, the animal totems – it has everything.

The Seven Directions

One could argue that there are indeed more directions (Heaven, Earth and Within, to name a few). If you prefer, here's a version that nods to all of them:

Oh, Spirit of the East, Land of the Rising Sun,
Of Air, the winds that blow across the lands
Of new beginnings each day, of open horizons
We ask for your wisdom and blessing here with us today
Spirit of the East, be here now!

Oh, Spirit of the South, place of Passion,
Of Fire, Creation, and Inspiration
Whose warm breath reminds us of summer days
Ignite our hearts with love.
We ask for your wisdom and blessing here with us today
Spirit of the South, be here now!

Oh, Spirit of the West, the land of the setting Sun,
Of Water and Autumn's whisper
Bless us with the peace that follows the harvest of a fruitful life
We ask for your wisdom and blessing here today
Spirit of the West, be here now!

Oh, Spirit of the North, place of Quiet,
Of Stillness, of Cave and Deep Earth
Place of thankfulness for the knowledge that comes to us with time
We ask for your wisdom and blessing here today
Spirit of the North, be here now!

Oh, Spirit of Mother Earth, you support us each day
Welcoming our roots deep into your heart
You nurture and guide us finding sustenance and support
Help us to give thanks always for your bounty

We ask for your wisdom and blessing here today
Spirit of Mother Earth, be here now!

Oh, Spirit of Father Sky, of the Angelic Realms
The countless stars of the night remind us that you are vast,
Beautiful and majestic beyond all of our knowing or understanding
Your Light shines upon the Earth, day and night, guiding our steps
We ask for your wisdom and blessing here today
Spirit of Father Sky, be here now!

Oh, Spirit of our Souls Within, place of Union, Love and Reverence
We are grateful for this gift of Life
And for the Love that guides our way
We open our hearts and join with all in Love.
Spirit of our Souls, be here now! It is begun.

Santo Daime Invocation Consecrating the Space

My favorite invocation is this one, from my Amazonian shamanic tradition:

In the Infinite Circle of the Divine Presence, which completely envelops me, I now affirm:

There is only one presence here – it is HARMONY, which creates a vibration in all hearts of happiness and joy. Whoever enters here will feel the vibration of Divine Harmony.

There is only one presence here – it is LOVE. God is love, which envelops all beings in a single feeling of unity. This sanctuary is filled with the presence of love. In Love, I live, I move, and I exist. Whoever enters here will feel the pure and holy Presence of Love.

There is only one presence here – it is TRUTH. All that exists here, all that is spoken here, all that is brought here is the expression of Truth. Whoever enters here will feel the Presence of Truth.

There is only one presence here – it is JUSTICE. Justice reigns in this sanctuary. Every act practiced here is ruled and inspired by Justice. Whoever enters here will feel the Presence of Justice.

There is only one presence here – it is the presence of God, who is GOODNESS. No evil can enter here. There is no evil in God. God, who is Goodness, dwells here. Whoever enters here will feel the Divine Presence of Goodness.

There is only one presence here – it is the presence of God, who is LIFE. God is the essential Life of all beings. He is the health of body and mind. Whoever enters here will feel the Divine Presence of Life and Health.

There is only one presence here – it is the presence of God, who is PROS-PERITY. God is Prosperity because She makes everything grow and prosper. God expresses Herself through the Prosperity of all that is carried out in Her name. Whoever enters here will feel the Divine Presence of Prosperity and Abundance.

Through the esoteric symbol of the Divine Wings, I am in harmonious vibration with the universal currents of Wisdom, Power, and Joy. The Presence of Divine Wisdom is manifested here. The Presence of Divine Joy is deeply felt by all those who enter here.

In the perfect communion between my lower self and my Higher Self, which is God in me, I consecrate this sanctuary to the perfect expression of all divine qualities which are in me and in all beings. The vibrations of my thoughts are the forces of God in me, which are stored here and hence radiated to all beings – thus establishing this place as a center of giving and receiving of all that is Good, Joyful and Prosperous.

— *CHURCH OF SANTO DAIME*

Ultimately, the purpose of all these prayers and invocations – as with all of our techniques – is to bring client and practitioner into a state of presence. These rituals are designed to attune the awareness to a higher frequency; to communicate directly with the subconscious; to create the space for acceptance, receptivity, and surrender; and to cue the alignment of our bodies and minds to the immediacy of the healing moment. Through these invocations, we signal the Universe of our readiness, and we let ourselves know at the deepest level that "It's on!"

Though these particular wordings are the ones we've incorporated, you're encouraged to work with whatever resonates in your own heart. The words themselves are secondary to the intention behind them. In some of my more dramatic shamanic expressions, I have been known to dispense with words entirely and conduct my prayers in Original Language (or vocables, if you prefer) – which alone can open a gap in our rational mental defenses big enough for Spirit to drive through.

Gratitude Prayer

Generally, we will also close our healing sessions with a prayer. I usually adapt the Healing Prayer above to one of Gratitude:

> *Father, Mother, Divine Spirit*
> *We thank you for joining with us in this moment of Perfect Healing*
> *We thank you for (Client's name) healing*
> *That shall forever be a demonstration*
> *Of Your Love, Compassion, and Will for her*
> *In her life and in this world*
> *And that she will forever be a witness to that*
> *We ask that our connection be clear*
> *And that whatever has come forward,*
> *Has been shared, transmitted, or received*
> *Shall be in service of the highest good*
> *For this we give our love and thanks*
> *And so it is*

One thing we don't do is ask Spirit for specific stuff. Our intention is simply to open ourselves to receive, and to thank Spirit for Her blessing.

I once asked one of my teachers: "If I'm looking for divine guidance, why don't I just flip a coin? I mean, God's in charge of the coin, too, right? So why not just put my trust in a coin flip?"

My teacher looked at me with compassion for my ignorance and asked, "Why would you limit God to only two options?"

We are asking to come into harmony with Divine will, not bend it to suit our own. All prayers are answered immediately, so the saying goes. Sometimes the answer is "Yes," sometimes "No," and sometimes "Not yet." What is the point of asking for Spirit's assistance while handcuffing Her with our own limitations and expectations, then dismissing Her when she doesn't adhere to our personal agenda?

Remember, this is only the beginning. Through coming present, through conscious breathing and the energetic techniques of The Touch and RAM Healing, we open a dialogue between ourselves, our clients, and the life force energy of Spirit – and then we learn to apply it in beneficial ways. Our bodies, our minds, and our hearts become the channels through which this boundless healing energy is expressed, and our hands become our instruments.

CHAPTER 13

The Touch and RAM Healing (Radiance Aesthesia Method) Core Methods

"He's got the whole world in his hands."

When I first started working with these methods, I had no formal training or technique whatsoever. I had had a powerful experience and demonstrations that led me to want to explore, develop, and expand my relationship with the healing power of Spirit. As I have continued working with these energies, I have confronted my own resistance and skepticism, which I believe is part of the process of growing and learning. I have been guided by an intention to deepen my own connection to Spirit through this work, a real curiosity about the value of these methods, and a devotion to being of spiritual service, to making a difference in the world.

Not long ago, I could not have imagined that I would have the privilege to work with people in this way, much less be writing a book about it. This, for me, is a true calling, which seems to require a whole new level of acceptance, trust, and surrender – ultimately nothing less than a complete realignment of myself with my Self. In many ways, I view the entire process as a rebirth.

So here we are. If you've made it this far with me, I know you feel an attraction to these principles already. I am certain that you experience some of the same sorts of doubts, uncertainties, and misidentifications that I have experienced as I have grown in this work. Perhaps these inner challenges are a necessary part of our education, evolution, and movement along this path. I encourage you to simply take any of those perceived issues with you, as you continue your journey of healing, and allow the presence and power of Spirit to guide you through your own awakening.

If you choose to work with these techniques, you will see results. They might be dramatic or subtle. They might look very different from how you thought they would look. They might involve the relief of symptoms and shifting or transformation of events, outcomes, personal feelings, habits, even relationships. You might be inspired to make adjustments in your own life as you come into resonance with the reality of living energy operating through you in service of healing.

Whatever happens, there is no way for you to fail. If you are at a point in your life where you can open yourself to the profound possibilities that these practices illuminate, you've already succeeded. These techniques work for healing the self and others. They are what we would call "perishable skills." It is not sufficient to just know about them; they must be practiced to be effective.

My master, Dr. Wu, once told me that the secret to mastery of Qi Gong is to keep doing it and doing it and doing it. My kung fu grandmaster, Don Baird, says it takes 10,000 repetitions of a move to begin to claim mastery of it.

Dr. Yuen put it this way: "When we first start doing this work, we do a great deal to achieve minimal results. As we progress, we do less and less to achieve more and more. Finally, as we become masters, we achieve our most dramatic results by doing nothing at all." Let's all bow in. It's time to train.

Practitioner Self Attunement
RAM Qi Gong for Healing Artists

This form derives from ancient t'ai chi, kung fu, and Qi Gong. The breath and movement exercises are specifically practiced to cultivate, harness, and express the healing energy of *qi (chi)* from Earth and Heaven. It stimulates clarity, presence, and calm, relaxed power, and conveys the usual benefits of this type of work in physical and mental health, cardiovascular function, and longevity. This Qi Gong is recommended as a daily practice. There is nothing to "figure out" about these movements. Simply perform them and allow them to speak directly to your body.

Beautiful Hands

The starting position for our breathing exercises is known as "Beautiful Hands." Stand squarely with your feet about shoulder width apart, palms open, and turned upward at waist level – at the *tan tien* (the energy center for *qi*, located a few inches below the navel area) – fingers and thumbs oriented toward one another, fingertips not quite touching, as though you're holding a bowl of water. As in all the basic Qi Gong stances, there is a slight forward tuck to the pelvis, and a slight contraction at the perineum. Hold this position and allow yourself to deepen into your breathing, establishing a slow, relaxed rhythm for a cycle of nine breaths. Breath is through the nose; the tongue remains in gentle contact with the roof of the mouth.

Beautiful Hands

Half Circle Breathing

Start in Beautiful Hands. As you inhale through the nose, raise your hands to the level of your heart – drawing energy upward from the Earth into your body. Pause and hold for a moment, with your hands at heart level, then turn your palms facing downward and exhale slowly, gently pressing down with your hands – sending energy back into the Earth. There is another brief pause in the breath, as you return to Beautiful Hands. The pattern is repeated for a cycle of nine breaths.

Half Circle Breathing

Full Circle Breathing

From Beautiful Hands: As you inhale, raise your hands up to the level of the heart, turning them all the way over, so that your palms face upward as you continue to raise your hands all the way up over your head (the "Happy Buddha" pose.) As you exhale, allow your hands to gently spread outward and "brush" downward to your sides – sending energy out beyond your body. There is no pause between the inhale and the exhale in this form. Breath is continuous all the way through the movement. Return to Beautiful Hands. Repeat for a cycle of nine breaths.

Full Circle Breathing

Split Circle Breathing

This form combines the first two. Begin in Beautiful Hands. On the inhale, both palms pull up from the waist to the level of the heart, where the hands split and separate. One hand continues rotating and moving upward and overhead (as in Full Circle Breathing), then continues to brush out and down to the side, the level of the heart, while the other hand rotates and pushes down the centerline of the body to the waist, where the hands come together again, palms up, in Beautiful Hands.

Repeat the movement, alternating the hands. Again, the form is repeated nine times on each side in a continuous flow with no pauses between breaths.

Split Circle Breathing

Apple Core Breathing

Begin in Beautiful Hands. On the inhale, the hands part and rise outward to the sides, palms up (gathering, receiving), and coming to a point overhead. On the exhale, both palms turn forward and descend together (sending) by simply dropping the elbows, allowing hands to return to the *tan tien*, where they turn upward and return to Beautiful Hands.

The form repeats for nine complete cycles, in one continuous breath, one continuous move.

Apple Core Breathing

Cloud Hands

From a well grounded stance, begin with the right arm shoulder high, elbow bent, forearm parallel to the ground, palm gently cupped and turned inward (a backhand block or strike position). Left hand is held at waist level, at the midline of the body, fingers and thumb extended toward the ground in a low sweep ("patting the child"). Your normal, natural breathing may or may not be synchronized with the movement. The body rotates 90 degrees to the right around the center body axis. In fluid motion, the hands "switch" high and low, with the left arm coming up into shoulder-high backhand strike pose and the right hand moving into a low sweep. The body rotates all the way to the left, where the hands switch back to the original position (right hand high, left hand low). The form repeats for a minimum of nine complete cycles, extended as desired. This is a most powerful and elegant form, with many subtle and fluid variations. Experiment with this movement in various arcs and rhythms. It works with wind chimes or tribal drums! This practice centers the practitioner, cultivates *qi* and expresses it beyond the body.

Cloud Hands

Dynamic Qi Activation

Whenever we perform these more physical movements, we want to make sure to protect our bodies, principally the knees, legs, feet, and lower back. Stand with your feet a little wider than hip width apart. Be conscious of your weight, shifting it to the outer edges of the feet, so as to protect your knees, which are slightly bent, by maintaining a widened space between your legs. This position prevents the knees and legs from buckling inward toward each other and the inner arches from collapsing. The weight is also balanced in the center of the feet – not too much weight on the heels or metatarsal bones. Tuck in your pelvis and sacrum slightly to avoid arching the lower back. The arms are rounded in front of you with the fingertips of one hand pointing toward the fingertips of the other.

Except for the slight pelvic tilt, the back is straight, the neck is stretched, and the head is suspended upward, as if from an invisible cord attached to the top of the head. The eyes are softly focused, at about a 45° angle toward the ground. This classic, grounded "barrel stance" is a central alignment feature of *Eternal Spring Chi Kung* by Seymour Koblin, HHP – Founder of the International College of Holistic Studies, from whose work these following forms derive.

Three Centered Breathing

This method combines a three-part *Pranayama* yogic breath with a dynamic Qi Gong/t'ai chi movement.

FIRST BREATH IN: Reach down and "scoop" *qi* from Mother Earth, and pull it into your *tan tien*. Pull breath into your belly.

SECOND BREATH IN: Open the chest, arms, and hands up and out, radiating *qi* outward and upward. Pull breath into the chest.

THIRD BREATH IN: Extend your arms all the way overhead, "capturing *qi*" from Heaven. Maintain the inhale, bringing your hands together like a prayer above your head and tilting your head back slightly, gazing up at your hands. At this point, your body is like an arrow aiming upward toward the heavens. Pull breath into the head.

LONG, SLOW BREATH OUT: Slowly exhale, lowering your prayer hands down in front of you while bending your knees and transporting *qi* from the heavens down through your body, releasing and letting go. This movement returns *qi* to the Earth for recirculation, with your fingertips finally pointed to and resting on the ground.

Repeat this sequence 18 times. These movements are fluid, a flow from one to the other, with a slight pause at the end of the inhale and exhale. Three Centered Breathing honors our inner connection with life force energy by bringing *qi* into our bodies and then restoring it to Heaven and Earth.

Three Centered Breathing

Sleeping Lion

Bend from below the navel with arms folded. Allow the weight of your upper torso to stretch the backs of your legs as gravity elongates your vertebral column. Breathe slowly and hold. Eventually your legs will become more flexible and you will bend forward more easily. The neck maintains the same position as our standing postures. We simply bend below the navel at the Tan Tien. Everything else stays in normal alignment.

Sleeping Lion

Roaring Lion

On the inhale, voice the sound "HING" as you lean back and lift the arms. On the exhale, voice the sound "HAR" as you lean forward while pushing your fingers into the Tan Tien. The inhale sends the diaphragm down, and the fingers pushing into the Tan Tien stimulate the exhale and the rising of the diaphragm. Allow the air to flow freely through the throat (don't engage the vocal cords). Practice 18 times in rapid succession, followed by slowing the breath in a standing position with the hands over the Tan Tien.

Roaring Lion

Dragon Claw

Stretch, Claw, Fist, tightening the fingers throughout the three stages of Dragon Claw. The move is performed dynamically to energize the entire body while maintaining a normal, relaxed breathing rhythm. Powerfully and specifically activates and channels energy through the hands – and makes your hands incredibly strong! Great for bodyworkers!

Dragon Claw

Barrel Stance

Completing our cycles of breathing and movement exercises, we now come into a strong, silent, relaxed grounded Barrel Stance, and just allow ourselves to "be the witness."

Barrel Stance

Light Circles

Hold a well-balanced Barrel Stance, feet hip to shoulder width apart, knees bent, pelvis tucked slightly forward, pelvic floor muscles slightly contracted, tongue resting against the roof of the mouth, breathing slowly through the nose. Arms held in a circle in front of the body as though "holding a barrel" (of energy!). Hands cupped gently, fingers oriented toward each other.

There should now be lots of *qi* moving in your body. Now it's time to start intensifying, brightening it, directing it. In our Radiance Aesthesia Method, we work with a visualized form of *qi* expressed as light.

While holding your Barrel Stance, visualize your crown chakra opening and a column of light coming directly in through the top of your head. This is pure, crystal clear, white light. As we progress, we will work with various frequencies and expressions of light, but for this preparatory clearing and energizing process, we'll work with white light.

When I first started working with Spirit light, it was always white light. I still use white light often, since it is so pure and clear, so easy to see, experience, and channel. As my own work deepened through experience, I came into the awareness that what we perceive as white light is really an amalgam of every color and frequency imaginable.

When I tune in to the Spirit light now, I first perceive white light, which then separates into its infinite components and appears as an interdimensional grid of color, expressed as a dynamic, living spectrum – interwoven fractals, reflections within reflections, sharply defined geometric shapes or soft, subtle waves of shimmering color, similar in appearance to the Northern Lights.

The appearance of this Spirit light is infinitely variable, each color and frequency perfectly tuned to the aspect of healing for which it is intended. You will come to work with Spirit Light in all its subtle and brilliant variations and expressions as you move forward. White light is all light combined, the synthesis of all the components of the Radiance. It is extremely powerful, clear, and simple, which makes it perfect for our current purposes.

Pull in the white light through the top of your head. Let it descend into your heart chakra. When it reaches your heart, the Spirit light increases in radiance, traveling in an arc down your right arm to your right hand (your "sending" hand) across the space to your left hand (your "receiving" hand), up your left arm and back through your heart center. As it circles through your heart and hands, the Spirit light continuously brightens and intensifies – until you are fully illuminated; until "you," in effect, disappear; until there's only the light.

You're fully energized, in a relaxed state, consciously directing energy flow. You're almost ready to go to work. There's sort of a preflight checklist, like switching on different circuits of consciousness: You want to *increase* feeling, perception, intuition, and creativity and *decrease* linear thinking. You want to increase your neutrality – be free of judgment and criticism, be fearless, bodiless, boundless. You want to increase your self-confidence and trust. These enhancements are accomplished through making energetic adjustments or corrections – the simple, direct act of bringing the qualities into consciousness and "switching" them in the desired direction to increase or decrease their energetic influence. Now, fully lit up and all switched on, it's time to go to work.

Self Clearing

"Self clearing" is an essential part of our practice. We self clear before, after, and between each major phase of our treatment session. This helps clear any material or obstruction we might be carrying into our session or taking on empathically from our client. From a well-grounded stance, feet shoulder width apart, knees bent, pelvic floor muscles lightly tucked, hands hanging at the sides, fingers extended downward toward the Earth, breathing consciously; we pull in the column of Spirit light (white or rainbow light) through the crown chakra and let it swirl and clear downward through the body, radiating outward beyond the confines of the body, downward through the arms and legs, flowing out from the hands and feet into the Earth (there to be used in service of regrowth, regeneration, and rebirth!), joining Heaven and Earth with a column of light that travels all the way through our bodies.

NOTE: This is an *essential* practice for practitioners of The Touch and should be practiced frequently throughout the day.

Self Clearing

Radiance Aesthesia Method

Client Preparation

When working hands on, we usually have our client sit on a simple, support-ive, straight-backed chair. This facilitates breathing and encourages alignment and optimal function of the body's energy centers. A client also might be lying down, or in any position of comfort. Yogis love their *asanas* (poses). We call in the Spirit light together, and recognize the sacredness of this moment. We start with a brief consultation, just to find out what's going on, and to estab-lish a bond of trust and love. We start to get a sense of the issue, its chronic and current condition, and how it's affecting the client at different levels – physical, mental, emotional, psychological, spiritual.

Energy Posture

We'll have the client take an energetic posture in the chair: feet on the floor, toes pointed slightly toward each other, hands on the lap, palms up, fingers oriented toward one another. This position encourages the fresh *qi* to remain in the system and not leak out. The important thing is that this all be done effortlessly and without muscular tension, using a relaxed, easy, well-supported posture. In fact, this dynamic of unforced, relaxed, gentle, effortless energy is what we're after throughout every part of the session in particular, and the work in general.

Energy Posture

93

As the client closes her eyes, we guide her – and ourselves – into a Conscious Breathing pattern. Use one of those described earlier, such as One-Pointed Breathing, Spinal Breathing, Forward Circle Breathing, Reverse Circle Breathing, or Microcosmic Orbits.

Once the primary breathing pattern has been established, we instruct the client to illuminate the path of the breath with a light the color of their own choosing. All of these patterns produce different energetic results. Of the circular patterns, the most prevalent is Forward Circle Breathing. It features continuous forward turning circularity – a powerful metaphor for positive change – and requires a counterintuitive form of attention, which helps override mental interference and also helps keep energy in the system.

Now, as the client falls into this easy, natural, unforced breathing rhythm, we'll guide her through a process of opening her *chakras* (energy centers). During this time, I am also opening my energy centers and connecting with the client through them. Beginning at the *root chakra* (the first chakra), we move up through our bodies – through the reproductive center or *sacral chakra* (the second chakra), the *solar plexus chakra* (the third chakra), the *heart chakra* (the fourth chakra), the *throat chakra* (the fifth chakra), the *third eye chakra* (the sixth chakra), and the top of the head or *crown chakra* (the seventh chakra).

At each level we encourage letting go of any muscular tension or holding, any doubt, anxiety, worry, conflict, or debris of any kind, anything that might obstruct the free flow of energy; we just let go now, just let go. The chakras open easily, naturally, without force, just like the iris of a lens. The root and the crown open downward and upward, respectively. The other five chakras open to the front and rear, across the spine. At each level, we illuminate and energize the center with Spirit light.

1st Chakra (Root) – Red
2nd Chakra (Reproductive/Sacral) – Orange
3rd Chakra (Power Center – Solar Plexus) – Yellow
4th Chakra (Heart, Spirit) – Green
5th Chakra (Throat, Emotions, Communication) – Turquoise
6th Chakra (Third Eye, Psychic, Intuitive) – Indigo Blue
7th Chakra (Crown, Heavenly Connection) – Purple

After clearing and connecting the chakras, move around to stand behind your client and place your hands on her shoulders. Your voice is soft and reassuring; your touch is extremely light, as you tune in to the current of energy traveling between you. You'll be amazed that this energy can feel so different with different people.

Once I have made this first hands-on contact, it's time to talk to Spirit. The prayer I use consistently is this one, which is a version of the Healing Prayer my rescuers on the mountain spoke over me.

Father, Mother, Divine Spirit
We join with you now in this moment of Perfect Healing
We ask for Perfect Healing for (client's name)
That this healing shall forever be a demonstration
Of Your love, compassion and will for her
In her life and in this world
And that she will forever be a witness to that
We ask that our connection be clear
And that whatever comes forward,
Is shared, transmitted or received
Shall be in service of the highest good
For this we give our love and thanks
And so it is

Bright Water 1 and 2

This is without a doubt my favorite technique, and it is a core technique of the Radiance Aesthesia Method. It was taught to me by my master, Dr. Baolin Wu, and derives from an ancient, original Qi Gong technique from the White Cloud Monastery in China. It is simple, elegant, beautiful, and profoundly effective. I usually do it twice during a full session; the first time "sending" to the client and the second time "receiving." If I have only a short time to spend with someone (working with a large group or doing street healing) it is my go-to technique.

Stand behind the client, with your hands just lightly touching her shoulders. Visualize yourself "melting away" as you send your energy into the client as a cascading wave of clear, sparkling Bright Water. Follow its swirling, spiraling, hydraulic course through the body. Observe the flow, where it goes easily, and where it's blocked or obstructed. Apply consciousness to those areas until the water flows freely again. Follow the Bright Water in this way as it travels all the way through the client, finally draining out through her hands and feet and into the Earth, there to be used in service of renewal, regeneration, and rebirth.

Bright Water

Alternately, this method (Bright Water 2) can be applied in "reverse," where you take the client's energy into yourself as Bright Water, and work with it within your own body and energy field. The "sending" method is best for emotional/psychological issues; the "receiving" method is best for physical issues. The "receiving" mode can be quite challenging for the practitioner, as the physical obstructions encountered will often show up as transitory empathic symptoms or sensations within the practitioner's own body. Particularly when working with groups, it is not unusual (for me) to experience a round of physical and emotional purging following a session. You are advised to consistently self clear when employing this method.

The Bright Water technique seems to resonate naturally with most people, as it is a perfect way for life force energy to find its way through a crowded body system; it is a cleansing and restorative technique that operates at a very deep level. Clients report wonderful experiences and results with this technique. As I said, if I had only one to go with, this would be it. People also report that the sensation of aquatic movement stays with them sometimes for hours and days beyond the session.

Hands-On Healing

We've prepared ourselves and prepared our client. We've established first contact, and we've asked for Spirit's healing. We've activated our *qi,* and we've opened our energy centers. We've cleansed the energetic system with Bright Water. Now we're going to take all that fresh *qi* and flood those nice, clean energy centers with it!

The technique of applying *qi* in this way, circulating it directly through the energy centers, meridians, and other focal points, was passed on to me in various forms through Dr. Yuen, Dr. Wu, and my kung fu masters from the American Academy of Martial Arts, Grandmaster Steve Pisa and Premier Grandmaster Don Baird.

In each position, the touch is very light, mostly just energetic contact. Remain focused on that radiant loop of Spirit Light that's coming in through the top of your head and circulates through your heart and hands. Continue to brighten and intensify it as you move through the various positions, directing the flow of energy from your right hand, through the client's energy centers and focal points, into your left hand, then up your left arm and through your heart again in a swirling, shimmering Circle of Light.

Starting at the top of the head, circulate the energy through your hands, gently covering each region for as long as desired. When working with Light Circles through the chakras, the right hand remains a centimeter or so above each center, making no physical contact. Spend no more than a minute or two in each position:

Hand Positions

1. Right-Left crown hemispheres (top of the head)
2. Right-Left lateral hemispheres (sides of the head)
3. Right hand/third eye - left hand/cervical spine (or c-spine, back of the neck)
4. Right hand/throat - left hand/cervical spine
5. Right hand/heart - left hand/cervical spine
6. Right hand/solar plexus - left hand/cervical spine
7. Right hand/reproductive center - left hand/cervical spine
8. Right hand/root chakra - left hand/cervical spine
9. Both hands on palms
10. Both hands on knees
11. Both hands on ankles
12. Both hands on feet

13. Right hand/crown center – left hand/cervical spine (drawing energy up the spine)
14. Both hands on shoulders (downward grounding energy)

In each position, (except as noted in no.13 and no.14), the energy travels in a counter-clockwise loop through both practitioner and client. After all the key centers have been contacted, return to the area of initial concern (the chief complaint) and focus some additional attention there.

As noted, we generally work with our right hands "sending" and our left hands "receiving", though this can be varied just by changing the direction of the energetic visualization. This approach also applies to crystals, stones, wands, divining rods, pendulums, tuning forks, light pens, and so on (modalities under the collective heading "Radius Aesthesia," from which our method – in combination with Radiance lightwork – derives its name). Each one of these frequency transformers can be combined with energetic visualization.

When working with your hands, the touch is feather-light. These methods work with equal effectiveness without touching; in fact, as we'll see, they can be very effective at a distance. Feel and work with the energy. Deepen into your trust. Let your intuition guide you. This is a revelatory process that only grows with time and experience. Let it be revealed in you. Let it be revealed in those you touch. From the moment you step onto this path, your steps are guided. Trust the natural knowing that has brought you here, to do this work. Keep doing it. You have already succeeded. The healing already *is*. All you have to do is show up.

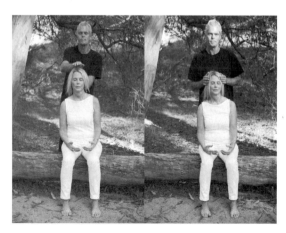

1. Crown Hemispheres   2. Lateral Hemispheres

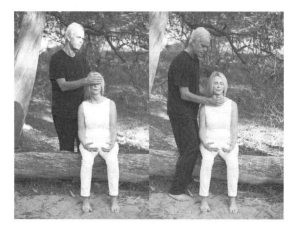

3. Third Eye   4. Throat

5. Heart   6. Solar Plexus

7. 2nd & 1st Chakra   8. Hands

10. Knees

12. Feet

13. Crown Chakra 14. Shoulders

Rising Rainbow

This method is a good choice for closing a session. While most of the techniques can be performed in relative silence, this one is spoken by the practitioner, a guided psychosynthesis meditation, which serves to bring the client back into an elevated, energized waking state.

Rising Rainbow

"Your attention and awareness focus on the system of roots that connect your body to the energy of the Earth. A pulse of bright red light travels up the roots and enters your body illuminating the first chakra at the base of your spine. As it swirls and spirals upward through your body core, it suddenly explodes outward in brilliant color, transforming into a bright rainbow of Spirit light, containing every color imaginable, every expression of light – shimmers and sparkles and fractals and rays, reflections within reflections, geometric shapes and soft, undulating waves like the Northern Lights, every frequency of this light perfectly tuned to Divine will for your personal healing.

Touching every system and cell of your body, mind, heart, and soul. Cleansing and clearing away any last traces of darkness or debris, as it travels upward into your heart center, radiating out from there, beyond the confines of your body, which now disappears completely until there is nothing but this light, this dazzling, intense, intelligent light, spiraling up and out, up through your throat chakra, your third eye chakra, your crown chakra, joining there with the Column of Light, all the way up, up into the Heavens, connecting there with your personal star, your life force, your Divine Source, the perfect union of Heaven and Earth in your body, right here, right now."

Soul Healing

This Radiance Aesthesia form honors the sacred connection between souls – between you and another person. It's like the lightworker's "Namaste." It is also an extremely powerful, moving, intimate way to share the blessing of healing. It is usually practiced at the very completion of the session, after both practitioner and client have been completely cleared. It is also often the form with which I close my workshops and healing circles, where all the participants share a moment of soul healing with one another.

Soul Healing

The form is essentially a light circle, performed in a sacred embrace. We approach one another, connecting through the left eye. We reach around each other with our left hands, placing them over the cervical spine at the back of the neck. We place our right hands directly over one another's heart chakras, as we deepen into the embrace. We hold this position for a time, simply sending light through our hearts and hands. We hold this position and allow our currents to run together, forming an energetic moebius loop, a bright infinity symbol that links us together in a timeless union with Spirit. Try this one with someone you love!

Distance and Remote Healing

"Distance healing" generally refers to working with someone who is not physically "in the room," but with whom we are in present-time contact by phone or Skype or webcam. "Remote healing" is when we're working with someone who may not be aware of our immediate connection, such as a distant family member, a person under medical sedation, or when we are asked to "send healing energy" to a loved one who is suffering.

I've personally seen some striking results from working in both of these modes. I'm not going to get into my limited discourse on quantum physics just yet (though I will later.) The general conclusion is that the pure, creative, intelligent energy we're working with is not bound by conventional physics, in the sense that its effects are instantaneous across time and space, causing science to reconsider the very nature of the universe. Is it holographic? Intelligent? Parallel? A unified organism?

Okay, that's a lot to digest. I can only say from my own observation and practice that I don't have a lot of reason to doubt the theory. For me, it comes down to, *does it work?* Bottom line: distance and remote protocols can be remarkably effective. You can achieve the same results in the same room or half a world away. I didn't make the law; I just try to live by it.

Any of the principal techniques discussed in this section can be practiced at a distance or remotely. Conscious Breathing, Chakra Clearing, Bright Water 1 and 2, Light Circles – they all lend themselves very well to distance work. Likewise, these techniques can be practiced with the participation of a "surrogate," a person who represents the person who is the object of the healing – usually someone who knows the person well and is willing to sit in for them. If you do work with a surrogate, remember to treat them with the same care, consideration, and thoroughness as you would give any client, and make sure to clear yourself and the surrogate completely.

Body of Light Healing

Another method for distance and remote work is called Body of Light Healing. It is similar in certain respects to Bright Water, particularly in its nonlinear elegance.

We perform our regular preparation, then call the client into our healing space. We visualize the client as a body of light – like a fiber-optic network of light energy with projections extending into the Earth, to the heavens, and in all directions at once. It is helpful to close or unfocus the eyes while experiencing the light body. We observe the patterns of light/color energy and look for areas of darkness, discoloration, asymmetry, density, or obstruction within the light body (which may be present in the location of the physical body or anywhere in the extended field of the light body), and we visualize the transformation of those frequencies into radiant, vibrant, healthy ones.

Body of Light Healing may be practiced with a surrogate, or as a distance or remote healing method.

Gratitude

Remember to thank Spirit. Make it a formal expression, a way of closing the Sacred Circle. A version of the one I use can be found in the earlier section on Prayers and Invocations. However you do it, do it. Remember always that it is *not you* doing the healing work; you serve something greater than yourself, whatever you want to call it, and however you choose to honor it. Your presence in the healing moment is a profound expression of your connection, even your devotion, to that greater something.

A Word on Practice

You might feel a bit cautious about reading a book, picking up a few techniques, and then running out to start throwing your hands on people. You're right to feel that way, and I'm not encouraging you to do that right away. I am encouraging you to *practice*. For that, you need a willing partner. This can be a friend or like-minded seeker. I encourage people who meet in our workshops or healing circles to connect and practice with each other.

Usually, it is best if your practice partner is *not* someone with whom you are in a relationship, a close family member, or someone you've known for a very long time. Our closest relationships are typically the most challenging when it comes to this work, for the simple reason that there's a lot of interfering noise from history and memory and everything we know, and all the decisions and judgments we've already made. Yes, it is perfectly possible to clear that material away and work effectively with a partner, loved one, or family member. It can also be confounding, frustrating, and stress inducing for both practice partners.

Far and away, the most willing and wonderful healing partners are animals! They have none of the baggage that impedes their human counterparts' capacity to receive and benefit from this type of work. They are completely open and available. They totally sense it and respond to it. I always marvel when I come into the home of a person with pets. When we start doing the work, the animals – particularly the cats – will invariably draw in and congregate around us in peaceful presence and "hold space." Most dramatically, I worked with a ranch woman in one of her pastures. One by one, we were encircled by three horses, equidistant from us and from one another, in perfect, sacred equine geometry.

One of my favorite and most naturally gifted students, Brittney, was extremely shy about working with people after she learned these techniques. She was on her way home to her parents' farm in Alabama for three weeks for the holidays. I guessed maybe they had some animals there. Oh yeah, for sure! So every day for three weeks, Brittney went out in the barnyard and threw her hands on dogs, cats, horses, chickens, goats, rabbits; I think there was even a pigeon or two. The next time I saw her was at one of our sacred circles in the desert, where, by the end of the night, Brittney was dressed in white at the head of the healing mat with people surrendering and releasing into her loving, inspired hands. In the Taoist Qi Gong tradition of my master, Dr. Wu, initiates must work with animals for years before they are ever permitted to put their hands on a human being. Clear yourself with light before and after any session, whether your client has two legs or four!

CHAPTER 14

Beyond Space and Time –

S c o u t

"Karma is only in space-time and causality.
Your real Self resides non-locally."

— DEEPAK CHOPRA

I got a call from my sweet friend Monica. I've known her for years, from a spiritual center with which we're both connected. Our dear mutual friend Scout was in Hawaii and was very sick. Early reports were somewhat sketchy and uniformly serious – a debilitating gastrointestinal illness with dire fore-warnings from the initial assessment.

Scout was going in for tests the following week. Monica asked me if I would please send some healing energy his way. I said, absolutely. I had been working with a remote healing protocol: healing at a distance, where the sub-ject is unaware of the work being done. I told Monica I wanted to work this way with Scout. I asked her not to tell him but to keep tabs on him and let me know how he was doing.

The next day, I climbed several miles and a couple thousand feet up to the top of Eagle Rock in Topanga State Park near my home. It was a surre-ally beautiful spring day – wildflowers blanketing the hillsides in purple and gold; the view across the Pacific, infinite. I did some Qi Gong, then sat on the highest ledge, facing west, toward where I knew Scout to be. I knew it didn't really matter which way I was facing, but that's what I did. I spent some time breathing, meditating, and just clearing myself. Then, when I was ready, I sent myself to Hawaii. I found my friend Scout on a beach and touched down behind him. He seemed to sense something, stirred, looked around. He didn't see me and turned back to his contemplation of the ocean before us, where some dolphins were playing just offshore.

I stood behind Scout, placed my hands on his head, connecting with his energy. At once I felt a surge of emotional turbulence and noticed my friend was crying. I sent him beautiful, calming light and the soothing sounds of harmonic resonance. His body began to relax. His eyes drifted shut. He began to sway softly, as though to some gentle inner rhythm.

Just exactly as I would've done had I been physically present with him, I went through a complete session with Scout, bringing in the Spirit light, praying and invoking Spirit, scanning him at different levels for energetic weaknesses, making energetic corrections as needed, clearing and cleansing him with Bright Water, circulating fresh *qi* through his energy centers, making enhancing elemental corrections, infusing him with perfect healing.

I worked with Scout for more than an hour. A remote session of this length is rare, since it's my impression that the healing takes place in an "instant out of time." I wanted to be thorough – not because Spirit needed to be shown where to go, but so that I would know where I had been. The session concluded, as always, with an expression of gratitude to Spirit. My eyes blinked open, and I was back on top of my rock in Topanga. The sun was setting as I started my long hike back to the car.

A couple of days later, I got a call from Monica. Scout's symptoms had improved, and he was feeling better. By the following week, he felt fine. His tests came back negative for anything scary, and his symptoms did not return.

This encounter illustrates some of the deeper principles of this sort of healing. Here, we're simply playing a part in a larger cosmic dance. It is as though the Universe empowers us with free will so that we may choose to find our way to exactly where it wants us at any given moment. We're terminals, connecting points in a massive grid of moving energy shaped by forces unseen and unknown. Scout's case, like many healing encounters, represents a confluence of energies, all contributing to what we might refer to as an "optimal outcome."

Yes, it is possible to analyze, deconstruct, devalue, and invalidate these experiences. Some of us live our entire lives doing this automatically, usually out of fear, unable to open ourselves to an expanded conception of what's really going on.

This work, however, asks us not to do that. It asks us, instead, to continue opening ourselves to it, to offer ourselves as conduits for it, to learn to trust and rely on our intuition, our empathy, our natural knowing. It asks that we lift ourselves beyond a linear interpretation of reality, to embrace an expanded definition of ourselves. It asks us to live and work in the realm of what's possible, to accept that we are spiritually much greater than we pretend to be. Maybe we're a lot farther down this wormhole than we realize. As mathematical cosmologist Brian Swimme articulates, "Fourteen billion years of evolution, and we're the latest model."

Suppose we allow that we are interdimensional beings united by a living energy field that is both intelligent and compassionate. As "beings," we are organized elemental expressions of that unified energy, microcosms of the Totality, essentially connected to one another across countless expressions and emanations. We are in a constant state of interaction with these "other" expressions of ourselves – which exist simultaneously in alternate vibrational states. We sometimes call them "ascended masters," "angels," "guides," or "beings of light."

These relationships exist along a spectrum that includes higher and lower frequencies, which could roughly be translated to mean higher and lower states of consciousness. Our current physical manifestation, the one defined by our point of view relative to our senses, resides somewhere along the spectrum of our total experience, neither at what we call the top or the bottom. It's probably inaccurate to perceive it in any sort of linear arrangement, since it's probably better expressed as a continuum, but all of those vibrational states affect us right here right now.

The mathematics for these interdependent relationships exist; we just haven't mastered them yet. Theoretical physics is lighting the way. In terms of the mind's influence over physical reality, our best science may still be like apes throwing bones at the sky. The perception that we are separate from each other – or from the Source that animates us – is an illusion; we interact and influence each other at all levels, all the time.

As we deepen in this work, as we relinquish our sense of control and simply *allow*, we learn to accept the improbable as routine and the impossible as just another opportunity for growth. This process is always revealing, always surprising, never boring. It will take you places you might never have imagined. It has most assuredly done that for me.

CHAPTER 15

"You Give Me Fever" –

Mike

"Out beyond ideas of right-doing and wrong-doing
There is a field.
I'll meet you there"

— RUMI

It was a cool, gray day at the retreat, and in my bones I could feel the cold push of winter. I was feeling a bit out of sorts, kind of disconnected and alone, far away and out of touch with the people in my life – "a yearning undefined," as the song says. Aimlessly, I wandered under the oaks to a clearing, pausing for a time to watch the ravens circle overhead. I thought of their association with death and felt the chill of my own mortality. Even healers get the blues.

As if on cue, my friend Ed appeared and snagged my arm.

"Come on," he said, "I need you right now."

"What's up?"

"We're going to the rock."

Ed was my closest friend at the retreat – a devout Christian guy with an open mind and heart, a brilliant drummer with a built-in backbeat, a minister's son who shared my passions for spiritual healing and bootleg burritos from the Mexican joint down the road. Man does not live by rice and veggies alone.

We started up the trail to the rock. Ed filled me in on the way.

Mike was the father of Ed's oldest childhood friend, and Mike had been something of a second father to Ed growing up. Not that Ed needed a surrogate, as his own parents were both permanent, beautiful fixtures in his life – a loving, devoted, compassionate couple whose lives revolved around their service to God and to others.

In the last few days, Mike had become suddenly and critically ill with a major systemic infection, the details of which were somewhat unclear. He had been found unconscious at his home, burning up with a massive fever, which was reported to be 113 degrees. No, that is not a typo: 113 degrees!

I stared at Ed. Neither of us had ever heard of an adult with a fever anywhere near that level. My own medical training screamed that there was no way a human being could survive such a temperature; and even if it were possible, they would doubtless sustain massive organ failure and brain damage. Mike was currently packed in ice at a major hospital, listed as extremely critical, vacillating between unresponsive and delirious, undergoing radical IV antibiotic therapy.

By all accounts, his prognosis was uniformly grim. We had no reason to believe that a couple of guys sending light from a rock 50 miles away would have any effect whatsoever. So, in the pure essence of the healer's mindset – total commitment to the process and total detachment from the results – we went for it.

I knew little about Mike, except that he existed, his name, age and location, and that he was a dear friend of my dear friend. In pilot talk, I was flying on instruments alone.

We climbed to the rock, sat down, oriented ourselves toward where Mike was (an automatic adjustment to physical world reality having nothing to do with the healing realm, for in the field of light, there is no direction or distance), and we went to work.

Though it was the first time for either of us to work in tandem with another healer, there was a natural synergy between Ed and me that seemed to far exceed the sum of its human parts. We said our prayers, synchronized our breathing, opened our chakras, and dived together into an interdimensional vortex, which spun us both out somewhere beyond the edges of space-time.

As I have previously described, heightened visual and auditory experiences are common in this context. I could hear Ed's syncopated chanting, could hear my own voice echoing in some ancient language, where understanding was both implied and immaterial, where the syllables were only symbols of something infinitely larger than the two of us. Somewhere beneath the blend of our voices was a subtle percussive current on which our energies rode like waves.

I was still remotely aware of my body in contact with the cool granite of our sacred rock somewhere in God's country, but I soon found my consciousness transported to another place entirely – inside a cavernous city hospital, in the Intensive Care Unit beside Mike's bed. He was packed in ice like seafood, eyes rolled back and glazed over, hooked up to all manner of IV lines and monitors that clicked, dripped, beeped, and buzzed softly.

Across from me, Ed stood by like a guardian spirit – eyes closed, hands open, sending waves of energy into the still, silent body of his friend. I continued my fantastic voyage deep inside, my attention and awareness penetrating Mike's body through the top of his head and into the interwoven network of neurons of his central nervous system, the power grid and portal to all levels of the human being.

I began a detailed process of scanning, testing, and correcting energetic weaknesses within Mike's whole being, a journey that took me into multiple levels of his experience: physical, mental, emotional, psychological, spiritual – into his fears, traumas, and memories. I felt myself deeply connecting with this man, felt his pain and terror, the searing heat of his fever, and the bone-chilling cold of the ice intervention. I felt my own body shaking and a wave of powerful emotions traveling through me. I have learned not to fear this phenomenon, as I frequently have the experience of processing the suffering of others through my own body and psyche as I do this work.

I worked top down through his major organs, lymphatic system, and cellular structures, through widespread inflammation, pockets of stagnation and parasitic infestation. I worked to clear chemical, pharmacological, and environmental toxins. I focused on his subcellular composition, on the permeability of his cellular membranes, on the free exchange of nutrients and the elimination of waste products, right down to the double-helix spiral of his DNA. I did enhancing elemental corrections with oxygen, water, carbon, glucose, and trace minerals. I sent light circles through his chakras and did bidirectional rounds of Bright Water with him.

Basically, I threw the whole book at Mike. I had nothing to lose. I took this very detailed approach not because of any great plan or predetermined methodology, but because it was the only path that revealed itself in the course of the session. We'll talk at length about Intuitive Scanning in a later chapter.

After a while, I came back into myself. My eyes blinked open, and I found myself back up on the rock with Ed beside me, still in meditation. He seemed to sense my return, and he, too, opened his eyes. We sat in silence for a long time. I glanced at my watch. An hour and a half had passed.

It was several days before we got word on Mike's condition – the cost of being off the grid without phones or computer communications, like waiting for the Pony Express to deliver a message to some remote outpost.

Ed's parents came out with the first report. Mike had stabilized, his fever had broken, and his temperature was back to normal. He was still in the hospital, had been moved out of the ICU, was still exhibiting signs of confusion and some short-term memory impairment and altered mental status, but he recognized his wife and family and was fully responsive and no longer delirious. He was being kept for additional observation and testing to determine the nature and extent of any functional abnormalities or possible brain damage.

Considering the severity of his previous condition, his prognosis was cautiously optimistic. Ed and I continued to hold Mike in our healing space, praying for him daily and sending him light during our morning meditations. Another several days passed before we got a visit from Ed's parents. Mike had gone home from the hospital. There were no apparent problems in his organic chemistry, his memory had returned, and there were no appreciable signs of brain damage. For all intents and purposes, Mike was completely normal. He had come through his harrowing ordeal virtually unscathed.

Ed and I allowed ourselves a high five and a chicken burrito in celebration, both of us clear that what we were celebrating was a demonstration of Divine intervention, grateful that, in our own small way, we had been privileged to participate.

CHAPTER 16

Sacred Medicine

"Mother of my Soul; Soul to set me free
You have given me all that I need to help me see."
— SHIMSHAI

Iam a Fire Monkey. My qualities are creativity, cleverness, and quickness. My avatar is Hanuman. My qualities are loyalty and service. My spirit-animal is the Jaguar, for silence, strength, and self reliance. My planetary ruler is Mercury, wing-footed messenger of the gods. My archetype is Hero. My ego fixation is "Go." My personal spirit guide is a light-being known to me as Bright Water, who has been described by those who have seen him as a "very tall angel with a nine-foot wingspan." I can't confirm this, since he always seems to stand behind me when I'm working. I am, however, acutely aware of his presence and guidance.

In my life, I have honored my father, and passed on our lineage to my son. Somewhere within me beats the heart of an ancient tribal warrior-shaman-medicine man. I'm guessing there's more than a bit of frontier preacher in there, too.

I've spent most of my adult life in decidedly *yang* pursuits, climbing and skiing big mountains and rescuing people in them, kayaking whitewater rivers and steep creeks, swimming, riding, and running distances that make me sick just to think about them. My most epic athletic performances have come since my injury, one step, one stroke, one turn of the crank at a time. I've sacrificed my body countless times in pursuit of adrenaline. I know how to fight, and I have learned both the advantages and limitations of physical force. I've achieved success in a carnivorously competitive, male-dominated business. I've walked through fire and emerged stronger for it. When the shit goes down, I'm a brother you want on your side. My record would suggest that I'm something of a guy's guy, an assessment with which I would humbly concur.

That being said, I'm a man deeply in touch with my inner woman. This work has deepened my sensitivity, my empathy, my caring and concern for others. It has enhanced my ability to be present, to be receptive, to listen, feel, and understand. When I was in Spiritual Psychology, my class was composed of about 70 percent amazing women, whose divine presence and energy were nothing short of a lifesaver for me during a time of intense, turbulent personal growth. I used to joke that I was so in touch with my feminine side, my period had synched up with my classmates.

Most of my friends are women. Most of my clients are women. My most revered teachers are women. The most skilled, dedicated, and toughest athletes I know are women. The flat-out smartest people I know are women. The healing artists and practitioners I most admire are women. Most of the help I needed when I was recovering came from women. My most influential instructors in outdoor rescue are all women. By far, the strongest and most inspirational people I know are women. The most rewarding, revealing, and challenging relationships of my life are with women. All the mothers I know, including my own, are women. I'm sure they all talk about me at their secret meetings.

United as one, divine masculine and feminine, lover and beloved, Guardian and Goddess, Shaman, Warrior, Priestess, Seeker, we enter Her temple together. Over the meadow and through the woods to Grandmother's house we go… We're talking here about *entheogens* – ancient Earth medicines that "generate the God within." They are *not* a part of this method, and this is *not* an endorsement or recommendation. In fact, I strongly recommend *against* their use in any but the safest and most sacred of settings, with skillful guidance and watchful protection, as well as the close proximity of advanced medical care.

These plant medicines must be approached with great respect and clear intentions. The body must be carefully cleansed, detoxified, and prepared, and must be free of any pharmacological contraindications. Sufficient time and reflection must bracket these experiences. Perspective must be gained in order to assimilate and integrate the lessons they teach. Properly safeguarded and administered, they are powerful psychotherapeutic adjuncts and messengers for spiritual revelation. There's also ample evidence of their value in the treatment of certain substance abuse disorders, depression, and post-traumatic stress disorder (PTSD). In the context of health and healing, their potential cannot be ignored.

Specific to the category, we find Ayahuasca, ibogaine, peyote, psilocybin, and *amanita muscaria* mushrooms, DMT, and 5-MEO-DMT. All are classified in the United States as Schedule 1 substances, assigning to them no medical value and a high potential for abuse – in the same general category as heroin and methamphetamine.

To lump these sacred teachers in with the deadliest, most life-sucking venoms known to mankind is to miss their point entirely, and highlights a system shadowed by fear and ignorance. Anyone who thinks these medicines have a high abuse potential has never spent a night purging into a pail. To say that I disagree with the current laws that regulate the sovereignty of our consciousness would be a gross understatement.

I feel the challenge of separating my personal, emotional connection to this subject from my reporter's objective observation. I have experienced profound healing and remarkable growth and change from my work with plant medicines. The subject is so important and far reaching that it seems nearly impossible to do it justice. But I shall attempt to add my voice to the chorus.

Specific to the topic of this book – healing with Spirit energy – their teachings have awakened in me a much deeper awareness of and relationship with the living energies we encounter in this line of work. The things I once considered extraordinary, esoteric, even unreal, are now just another night at the office.

All of our pain, fear, worry, doubt, depression, self-judgment, self-condemnation, self-punishment, all of our anger, violence, inhumanity, guilt and anguish, our sense of lack, isolation, alienation, loneliness, yearning – all of these prisons are built on the bottomless quicksand of consciousness that results from our disconnection from Divine Source.

All who would be free of these prisons must heal that relationship, must clear the impediments, obstructions and debris that block the full expression of Divine presence. This requires deep self-examination and courageous surrender, a vision quest, a willingness to wander through the dark woods of our inner world toward the bright radiance of our true nature. We must meet and master our inner demons. We must encounter our Spirit guides and open our hearts to their wisdom. We must make changes in our lives based on what we learn from them. We must walk our talk. We must fall in love with ourselves again. Trust me, it's better the second time around.

Yes, the state of enlightened consciousness can, and ultimately must, be achieved through methods other than sacred medicines – breath, prayer, meditation, yoga, spiritual practice, and service. But they are here – and have been here since the Dawn of Reason – for exactly that purpose. Mankind has always been driven to know God. It is, in fact, our ultimate driving motivation as human beings. It is the essential destination on our spiritual path. I know you recognize this because, well, here you are. If you didn't, you'd have put this book down a long time ago.

The medicines are here to serve our collective awakening. Their wisdom is ancient, timeless, eternal. They are not "the answer," but they open our hearts to the question. They provide access to realms of information not available through ordinary means. Their lessons are not always easy and not always comfortable. If you let them, they will guide you to a new level of truth, authenticity, meaning, purpose, accountability, and responsibility. They will instruct you in who you are. They will remind you that love is your essence. What you do with that knowledge is up to you.

For our purposes here, our interest lies in their potential as agents of personal healing – both self-healing and facilitating healing in others – as well as catalysts for spiritual growth and transformation. The accounts are limited to the frame of direct personal experience. As I have deepened in my work with these teachers, I've been opened to a deeper view, to a range of possibilities I would have never imagined before.

The two stories that follow are from my early experiences with entheogens in this context. The later material is from, well, later. After spending many nights around a healing mat in a sacred *cura*, I want to take you there. Fasten your seat belt.

Paolo

I got a call from my friend Paolo. We hadn't spoken for a while. He'd been up in Northern California for some time, backpacking solo in the Sierras. He'd been on a vision quest. This was quite normal for Paolo. He would often head up into the mountains for weeks at a time on his personal spiritual journey.

Paolo was an amazing guy, a former itinerant shaman in Brazil. He invited me out for a hike in Ojai, one of our favorite ways to spend time together. I packed a daypack, including some mushrooms, and headed up there early Saturday morning. I was shocked when I saw my friend. He had lost 20 pounds since I saw him last and looked like a scarecrow – but his intense blue eyes and great smile were still the same as always.

I asked him what was up.

He didn't say much at first. "Come on," he said. "I'll tell you on the way."

We started up Matilija Canyon toward the falls. I noticed Paolo was moving much slower than I'd ever seen him move before. At 60-something, Paolo could normally blow me away with his trail pace. But not today. Today's progress was labored and slow.

We took the mushrooms at a stream crossing about an hour up the trail. Paolo began to open up. He told me a harrowing tale.

He'd been in the Sierra wilderness on a nine-day solo hike. A few days out, he started to feel sick. Vomiting and diarrhea. He thought it was *giardia*, the nasty little protozoan known to inhabit the waters of the Sierra Nevada. But Paolo was an old hand at treating his water, and he was carrying giardia medicine, which he started taking.

It didn't help. He couldn't hold down any food or water. He set a course for the nearest road, a couple of days away at best, and trudged off in that direction. The next day, he collapsed. He simply couldn't go on. He lay there like that through the heat of the day and the chill of the night.

When the sun came up the next day, Paolo knew he had a choice. He could either make one more attempt to go on, or he could die right there. Somehow, he rallied his failing body to get up and stumbled toward the steep incline that would lead to the road, still many miles away.

The rest of the journey was a blur. Paolo was found by the side of the road by a fisherman, who drove him to the nearest hospital. The mountain clinic was sparse at best, and nomadic shamans don't have the best medical plan. The doctors ruled out giardia, got Paolo rehydrated, and told him he should be tested for stomach cancer. That's actually why he was back in town. He was going in for tests the next week.

An introspective mood fell over our little party as we continued making our way up the rocky streambed. The mushrooms were starting to kick in. We reached a rock shelf about halfway up to the falls. Neither one of us felt much like going farther. We took a dip in the cold stream, then stretched out naked on the warm rocks. I closed my eyes and gave in to the first wave of heavy tripping.

When I opened my eyes again, Paolo was lying on his back, eyes closed, legs stretched out and crossed, arms spread out wide, palms turned upward. I experienced an instant psychedelic transference to an image of Christ on the cross. The impression was so clear and so intense that I scrambled at once to my knees and crawled toward it.

I found myself beside Paolo. As I looked at him, I got the very clear impression of a dark, pulsating mass on the midline of his body, between the sternum and the navel. I sat in silence beside him, cross-legged, and put my hands over this area, not touching him but just tuning in to this region of his body.

He sensed me there. His eyes flickered open. "Do your thing, man," he said with a smile.

I said my healing prayer and focused intently on Paolo's midsection, finally placing my hands on his body. I had this feeling of sudden, intense magnetic attraction, but something more – this feeling like something inside my friend's body was wrapping tentacles around my hands and trying to pull me in there with it.

Suddenly, all sense of separation between me and Paolo seemed to disappear. My hands somehow vanished inside his body; this dark thing was in there, too, and wasn't going down without a fight. As I wrestled with it, a deep guttural noise came grinding out of me – a primal, native warrior cry echoing off the walls of the canyon.

The "thing" came out of Paolo's body into my hands. It was, as imagined before, a dark, bloody, pulsating mass. With a frightening roar, I flung the horrible blob downstream. I could hear it gnashing and splashing as it was carried away by the current. I washed my hands in the stream and came back up beside Paolo. He was right where I'd left him. I put my hands on his stomach again, prayed again, and began to flood the area with white light. I pulled light energy in through the top of my head and sent it into Paolo's body through my hands. I could clearly see the bright connection of energy between us and its inner and outer emanations.

I finally removed my hands, which continued to glow, as did Paolo's stomach. The mushrooms mellowed out after awhile, and we were able to move well enough to make our way back down the canyon.

Over the next few days, Paolo's pain subsided. By the time he got his tests the following week, there was no trace of any cancer or immediate life-threatening issues in his body. He was soon healthy again, is now in his early seventies, and can still kick my ass with his hiking pace.

There has been ample research on the value of entheogens, such as mushrooms or Ayahuasca, to promote divinatory states conducive to healing. It is not my purpose here to recommend them; simply, to share another step along the path of my own awakening and to illustrate that there are many channels through which the energy of spiritual healing can be carried. As Neem Karoli Baba is quoted as saying, when Ram Dass gave him LSD, "It is not the true Avatar, but it is useful."

Healer, Heal Thyself

Paolo returned the favor some years later. Ever since my injury and miraculous healing 11 years before, I'd been tormented by pain – what the doctors called "chronic, intractable, central neuropathic pain." As I've mentioned previously, over the years I had tried virtually every pain management protocol you can name, except for having a pain pump surgically implanted – though that was on the table for a time.

After endless rounds of Western docs, Eastern docs, chiropractors, acupuncturists, pain docs, physical therapists, prolotherapists, and hypnotherapists, after untold dollars and countless hours and treatments and trips back and forth, I'd settled into the inconvenient habit of using pain pills to manage my pain.

While I was in many ways grateful for my pain, as I felt it awakened me and connected me compassionately to the suffering of others, I always felt it was kind of ironic. I mean, here I was, a guy who'd experienced a miracle healing first hand in my life, and through it discovered a gift for facilitating healing in others. I had made such extraordinary progress in so many other ways – in my movement, strength, flexibility, endurance, and overall health. Why couldn't I seem to heal myself of my pain? Pain pills? Really? For what – the rest of my life?

This issue played upon the very core of my doubts and kept me in the closet about my own healing gifts for years – though I did continue to study, learn, develop, practice, and grow.

Some years back, I came across a body of work associated with the plant spirit Ayahuasca and its application in shamanic healing among indigenous people of the Amazon over thousands of years. I really tuned in to this subject when I was looking for a story idea for a feature film, and ran across the work of Dr. Charles Grob, M.D., Ph.D., chief of Child and Adolescent Psychiatry at Harbor-UCLA Hospital, a totally mainstream shrink, if you will, whose research specialty is psychedelic therapy for the terminally ill.

The instant I tuned in to Charlie (in a front-page article in the *Daily Bruin* at UCLA, where my son Adam and I were psych students and where Charlie was on the medical school faculty,) I exclaimed, "That's it! That's my story."

I knew it immediately. It was one of those inspired moments that make me grateful to be a creative artist. I saw the whole movie in my head in a flash – the story, the characters, the visuals, the soundtrack, the timeless love, the message of peace and wisdom, the perfect platform for my own peculiar talents, built, as I like to say, at the intersection of creativity and healing.

I called Charlie's office that day and made an appointment to see him.

Charlie's a brilliant, engaging guy and heads the first federally sponsored, FDA/DEA–approved research program in the psychotherapeutic use of hallucinogens in 40 years. He is one of the original researchers who brought

Ayahuasca back from the Amazon in the eighties to study it formally. He's written several books on the subject, and I guess you'd call him a leading expert in the field.

Ever since I met Charlie, I'd been interested in Ayahuasca. I'd read about its remarkable curative effects for all kinds of physical and psychological disorders. I knew a number of people who had worked with it – clear, intelligent, successful people who told me of their life-changing experiences with the "Vine of the Spirits."

I'd been deeply involved with writing about it for my film project, but had always felt that I was missing an important piece of information because I hadn't tried it for myself. Not that I wouldn't have. I'd made several inquiries over the past few years with some of these people I knew – but it was always elusive, never quite there; maybe next month, that sort of thing.

Then, at our May class weekend in the masters program in Spiritual Psychology at the University of Santa Monica, I sat down in the facilitator's chair across from the client, a beautiful Brazilian girl who gave off this incredibly clear, sweet, connected vibe by which I was instantaneously energized. There was just something about her. We had an amazing trio session, loving and deep, toward the end of which she shared about her recent first experience with Ayahuasca. Listening to her, I "got" how powerful and transformational this experience had been – restorative, illuminating, profoundly healing. As I listened with my heart, I heard the plants calling me in the voice of this very special being in front of me.

I made a call to my friend Paolo the next day. The last time we had talked about it, he hadn't been working with the plants for years. But this time when I called, Paolo was like, "Sure, man. What time can you be here?"

That time turned out to be the next Saturday. I drove in from Las Vegas and was taking a shower in Paolo's funky backyard in Ojai by sundown. A short time later, we gathered under an awning. I sat on an old couch, wrapped in a zero-degree sleeping bag, an iron bucket nearby to manage the inevitable purge.

Paolo did a little ceremony and invocation as he poured the tea into a small cup and placed it in front of me. It was red or magenta, really, and viscous – not what I first pictured when I heard the word "tea." Paolo had cultivated the plants himself on Maui, giving years of his life to the process, and had spent weeks preparing and brewing in traditional, ancient, sacred ways the cup of Ayahuasca that now sat before me on an upended milk crate table.

Paolo looked at me, his eyes clear and endlessly blue, his look wise, deep, honoring. He asked me what I wanted this journey to be about. He told me to make my intention as simple and clear as possible, "so I could find it in the dark." The answer came forward without hesitation.

"That's an easy one for me," I said. "It's all about healing my pain."

Paolo sat for a moment in silence, a look of knowing passing across his intelligent face. Then he smiled, and with a little twinkle in his eyes, said, "Be careful what you ask for."

I drank my tea as the sun went down. Paolo sat nearby in masterful silence, just present, nothing less or more. Slowly, very subtly at first, I began to feel the medicine working its way through my body. It was not an uncomfortable sensation. Rather pleasant at first. I started to get little volts of energy traveling up my spine, swirling up and out the top of my head – reminding me of long-ago experiences with other psychoactives.

I started to chuckle a little bit at the sensation, a sort of deep, quiet laughter traveling upward through my chakras from the root to the crown. Paolo glanced up at me. I smiled and nodded and returned into the silence.

After an hour or so, I was feeling a bit anticlimactic. Despite those first few energy waves and a heightened awareness of light, color, and the softly echoing sounds of the neighborhood around us, I wasn't really coming on. I was aware of the medicine still traveling around inside me. I had the feeling that it was getting to know me as it located blocks and pockets of resistance inside my body. I thought about the weeks of road food, Vegas buffets, and takeout that had preceded this little trip to the Ojai mountains. I had a feeling like something was happening, but I was nowhere near where I wanted to be.

Paolo seemed to sense this. He came over to me, sat down, looked at me closely. He asked me how I was doing. "I feel like I'm barely scratching the surface," I said. He nodded, poured another cupful of the medicine, placed it in front of me. I drank my second cup of tea. I'm guessing it was 20 minutes before the effects of both cups of tea hit me all at once.

My surroundings began to move and breathe and crawl. Everything seemed to be charged with color, every particle of reality connected in swirling patterns of energy. The sounds of the village around us blended into a muffled symphony of human sounds: another Saturday night of partying, drinking, coughing, laughing, crying, fighting, screaming, slamming, screeching, roaring off into the darkness – but all so connected, so perfect and telling.

Things were getting darker. Those swirling patterns were becoming serpents and living spirits of the night. My guts were on fire now, but I still couldn't purge. I hung over the iron pail, praying for release, tripping on the spiral pattern at the bottom of the bucket. It got more and more intense. I began to feel trapped, targeted, under siege by living entities.

I had the sense of this *intelligence* inside me, scanning me on multiple levels, identifying, analyzing, classifying, and sending reinforcements to the parts inside that hurt. And, oh my God, I hurt so much. Not only from my so-called medical issues but from all the poisons in my body, all the abuse I've put it through, all the insults and injuries, all the tragedy and trauma, all the pain and heartache I'd carried for so long.

I was feeling afraid. Like I'd done something terribly wrong. Like I'd allowed this "thing" inside my body, and now here it was ripping me to shreds. Like, "Oh my God. What have I done?!"

I started to purge. Each wave was like a blessing from God. I remember whispering, "Oh, my God, Thank You," after each mighty hurl.

Paolo never moved, never reacted, just remained where he was in his stillness. Soon, I grabbed my bucket and headed inside to the corner mattress, where I'd put my pillows, water, and big fluffy comforter. I put the bucket nearby and crashed, clutching my pillows, pulling my comforter up around me, shivering.

The visuals were incredibly intense. I was flipping through dimensions like playing cards, seeing realities within realities, echoed and mirrored across countless expressions, emanations, and variations throughout space and time, soaring through the cosmos at quantum speeds, touching the edge of the void. At the same time, my body was going through an intense ordeal. The medicine had found its way to my lower GI tract. Between the bucket and the bathroom, my body went through an intense and powerful cleanse throughout the night. I don't want to get too much more graphic than that, but you get the idea.

Even as I went through my challenges, I always had the sense of this amazing, loving, compassionate, infinitely wise presence – a female – holding me, caring for me, making sure I was safe, nurturing me, guiding me, gently encouraging me to trust her, to surrender to her. I actually saw her, the one I call the Goddess, aka Grandmother – an interdimensional, cosmic feminine/Divine mother/lover/sister/queen. I experienced total love, total understanding, total forgiveness, total grace.

The medicine continued to overpower my internal resistance. My dance with the Vine lasted all night. I had no choice but to let go, to surrender absolutely, at last to lie there in the dark, tears of gratitude streaming down my face, whispering over and over: "Oh, my God, I love You. Oh, my God, I trust

You. I trust in Your will for me. I trust in Your plan for me. I give myself to You. Oh, my God, I trust You. Oh, my God, I love You… "

I know there were periods of sleep during the morning hours, after several intense hours when the medicine finished with my body. These periods of sleep were as lucid as when I was awake. It was a beautiful dream, where I knew I was the dreamer and also knew I was being dreamed by a dreamer who was also being dreamed. It was a dream where anything was possible, a realm unbound by Euclidean constraints. We were beings of pure light; we could be anything, anywhere, anytime. Then some music started to play, and we all danced.

The first rays of sunrise struck the window, shining on my face. My eyes flickered open. I lay there in silence for a while, feeling as though I was lying next to someone, holding her and being held. I felt completely safe, loved, and protected. I whispered those words again, "Oh, my God, I trust You."

After a while, I arose and stepped outside. The first thing I noticed was the dawn and the fine lingering mist hanging in the air. The fields around the house were steaming slightly, and the sun was on the rise. I stretched a bit, did a little Qi Gong, took inventory of my body. Despite my overnight ordeal, I was feeling very good – rested, refreshed, kind of clear and tingly. The world looked just as it did the day before, just somehow a bit brighter.

I noticed something else: my skin wasn't burning. This kind of weather would have normally set my skin on fire – the paradoxical sensation of a cool morning mist feeling like an army of fire ants. My body didn't hurt, despite the fact that I hadn't taken any pain meds in the last 18 hours. I moved around the yard a bit, feeling my body here and there, feeling barely a trace of the hypersensitivity and burning – the paraesthesia that had driven me mad for so long.

I immediately reduced my pain meds by 80 percent with no discomfort or ill effects of any kind. It is as though I simply shed the pain and the need to medicate it. Over the next couple of weeks, I eliminated them completely. I know that Ayahuasca is not what healed me; it only cleared the way for me, by compassionately decimating my resistance to the experience of divine surrender and absolute trust. And that is what healed me.

The Sacred Circle

Our brothers and sisters arrive in the desert before sunset. We greet each other joyfully, celebrating the reunion of our family of love. All have traveled great distances to this sacred space in the red rocks outside Joshua Tree National Park. We have prepared the temple for their arrival, and for tonight's *cura*.

Our gathering is protected as a religious sacrament of a Native American church. All who attend are required to be members. The ceremony dome is canvas and steel, transformed by loving hands into a warm, soft, colorful nest, dedicated to the Great Spirit and the Divine Mother . It is safe, inviting, womblike, part of a rainbow tradition – Tibet, India, the Amazon, the Native American desert, the Cradle of Man, Oceania, the Arabian Nights – all in confluence here on this stony plateau, perched on the edge of space and time.

Twenty-one souls will journey tonight, including our medicine woman, Valerie, and our guardians: two for the men, two for the women. Several of my close family are also present: my beloved Candice, my angel, my flame, 30 years a yogi and devoted spiritual practitioner; my son Adam, spiritual psychologist and virtuoso shamanic sound healer, and his love (then my dear friend and now my daughter-in-law) Aline, a sparkling Brazilian power source and a licensed holistic health practitioner.

My name's Doug. I'm one of your guardians. Places have been carefully arranged in a circle, with cushions and blankets and back jacks and paper towels and purge buckets. At the center of the dome lies the healing mat, where thousands have felt the touch of the Spirit of Ayahuasca, soon to be the epicenter of power in this place, now laden with drums, feathers, crystals, singing bowls.

We've all paid close attention to our *dieta*, maintaining for many days a diet free of animal protein, sugar, wheat, dairy, caffeine, alcohol, fermented foods, nuts, avocados – pretty much eating just fresh fruits and vegetables and drinking water. Those who have not will pay the price. Others have eliminated certain medications for weeks prior to tonight, particularly any medications containing a monoamine oxydase inhibitor (MAOI). This is extremely important, since the medicine already contains one, which acts to "unlock" or potentiate the DMT in Ayahuasca. Some who have sought to subvert this biochemical equation have canceled their return trips from Grandmother's house.

Most of us are dressed in white, many with accents of special colors. White signifies humility, receptivity, beginner's mind, the about-to-be-born. A few first-time travelers show up from LA in their city clothes, looking like they didn't get the memo. Someone has some extra yoga pants, someone else a sarong, a few colored silks… and before you know it, the newcomers look as trippy as the rest of us.

I'm barefoot as usual, in my white Indian cotton drawstring pants, fresh white v-neck t-shirt, off-white, fringed Tibetan silk shawl with chakra colored border stripes and fine gold threads. And my *mala*. Always my *mala*.

We pass the prayer books around, the spiral notebooks in which we each write our prayers and intentions for this ceremony. Some soft music plays as the circle comes together. Tonight, it's "Om in E," by David Childress. The mood turns thoughtful, introspective, meditative, as we reflect on what has brought us here tonight. What have we come here to heal, receive, give, and create? What guidance do we seek? What do we fear? What have we done? What do we do now? What must we resolve? Who are we praying for? How can we serve, grow, prosper, change? How do we get closer to the Divine within?

The books finally close and our prayers are placed upon the altar. Tonight, my intention is to serve the sacred circle with presence, focus, and love. I am asking Spirit for illumination and guidance along my healing path, to offer myself as a channel for the healing energy of Spirit, and to cleanse and clear any doubt, fear, conflicts, or obstructions to its full expression in my life. I ask for a gentle journey, to let Grandmother take me where she wants to take me, to show me what she wants to show me, and to give me the strength to carry out her wishes. And I'm totally up for a divine embrace.

Valerie opens the circle with binaural tones from a crystal sound bowl, followed by an invocation from her Native American tradition. She is the living vision of an Earth Goddess.

She speaks for a long time about the medicine, its history, tradition, and effects; about the nature of the journey we're about to take together; about its inner and outer visual and sensory properties; about "getting well" (purging); about some of the encounters we might experience with other beings, guides, or spirits; about the deep personal side of this work; about the synergy, empathy, and psychic connection within the group; about our extended tribe of light; and about the larger picture of what it might mean for people like us, everywhere, to come together and do this work, then take what we learn and implement it our lives and in this world; how together we might reach a critical mass that tips a fundamental shift in the story of humankind.

Valerie holds up a glass container full of blood-red Ayahuasca and gives a blessing. The bottle then passes to the next person and the next, around the circle.

We introduce ourselves, and share our prayers and intentions. We get to know and connect with each person, with their radiance as spiritual beings and their challenges as human beings. We get to identify with each other, to recognize our fellow travelers on the path of light, to hold one another in the highest vibration of love, understanding, and shared intention for the highest good. Everyone places a special offering or blessing directly into the medicine – love, joy, peace, harmony, health, laughter, compassion, illumination, surrender, strength.

At last, Valerie pours. One by one, the travelers kneel, consult, receive their first dose. Each is anointed with rose oil and whispered a special blessing by the *parfumera*. We return to our places in the circle, praying directly into our cups, for ourselves, our families, our brothers and sisters in the circle, for humanity and our Earth, for the grace of the Spirit of Ayahuasca. With a final blessing, we raise our cups.

Valerie smiles, radiant, a portrait of love and divine mischief. "My brothers, my sisters, *salud*!" We drink together as one.

I drink a solid working dose, about a "7," not intended to tear through the fabric of the space-time continuum but enough to gain admission to the field of light while maintaining my attention and focus on the needs of the group. The low lights come down into candle glow. We fall into silent meditation for a time. My eyes remain open. Valerie clears each of us; soft strokes with an eagle feather. There's a deepening heartbeat rhythm from a frame drum, mythical sounds from a water harp.

I focus – where else? – on my breathing, down and in, up and out. The medicine makes its way into my body, searching, snaking, looking for my inevitable resistances, checking, categorizing, and classifying – my internal organs, my spine, low back, knees, feet, neck, shoulders, hands, everywhere I hold tension, stress, pain. I feel my body shift into a more natural alignment.

More music now – divine musicians, celestial harmonies, ceremony songs. My breathing gets easier, deeper. I feel the medicine trickling down, from larger systems into smaller ones, intracellular scouts on patrol looking for invaders, working their way insistently into hidden pockets of irritation, inflammation, stagnation, toxicity. I chuckle to myself because I can actually *see* the little buggers, like double-helix roto-rooters, spinning and spiraling and slipping and slithering, seeding my innermost reaches with particles of light and consciousness.

Valerie sings the first of tonight's *icaros*, chanted prayers, this one alternating between *Quechua* and English. We're calling in the animals – the Jaguar, the Eagle, and the Condor, the Anaconda, the Dolphin, the Whale, the Monkey, the Hummingbird, the Wolf, and the Buffalo, and many, many more powerful animal totems and Earth spirits. By the time the *icaro* rounds the circle, even the Ant and Chicken have been summoned.

The energy in the dome is shifting and moving; the lights are different from before. Patterns are emerging. I can see spectral, transparent bands connecting everyone in the circle like spokes on a wheel. I see that we have always been connected; that we're sharing now in a timeless ritual of reconnection with what has always united us; that it lives here, right here, right now, in this place; that it is with us; that we are safe; that we are home.

I feel a sudden jolt. I look down, and I can see roots growing downward from the center of my body, twisting and writhing into the Earth, pushing deeper and deeper, through layers of the Earth, lost civilizations, dinosaur bones… all the way down, all the way down to the fire.

Intense heat rises through my whole body. I'm sweating, suffocating, I want to run outside, but I'm trapped, I'm rooted like a thousand-year-old tree. I watch myself sweat and want to run outside. I see my reflection like in a mirror in a public toilet. I look haggard, weary, dark circles under my eyes. My youth, my God, has anyone seen my youth?

I summon the strength, ready to rise, ready to bolt for the safety of the desert outside. Still, I don't move. I haven't moved the whole time. I'm still sitting quietly, eyes open, watchful. I find some other open eyes finding their way in the dark. Meaningful glances pass between us. I find my breath again. Follow it in, follow it out.

The music takes over, resonant strings, reed flute, frame drum, chimes, shamanic chanting, traditional *icaros*, intricate harmonies, subtle, shifting rhythms, Earth sounds. I know this sacred musician: it is my son, Adam. He's deep in his place, channeling the soundtrack of the soul. A wave of love and pride crashes over me. I have no words to describe it. My face is wet with tears, yet I am not crying. I close my eyes for a moment and ride the Spirit waves coming through my son.

Around the circle, things are heating up. There's some laughter, some sadness being released, some chanting and toning, some whispered prayers – a complex harmonic synergy punctuated by the human-animal sounds of purging.

I feel a surge of energy traveling up my spine. Breathing in deep, breathing out up the spine, and I'm suddenly riding that power wave, up and up through my own neural network. I can see the interwoven axons of my own inner circuitry as I accelerate upward, the G-forces pulling on my cheeks. I feel sick. I breathe through it, leveling off, feeling better, shifting into cruise mode. The medicine is going to be kind to me tonight.

Another sound hooks me, slingshots me back to Earth: my love, Candice, is going through an epic physical and emotional purge. To me, it sounds like something undead is coming out of her. I worry at once for her safety. My rescuer instincts are fully engaged.

I feel myself standing up, going to her, taking care of her, fixing everything. I don't move, but a quiet glance passes between me and one of the female guardians nearby, who smiles and calmly watches over my love. Still, I can't help but feel what she feels. I love her. I share her prayers and intentions. I know how deeply she does her work. She's doing it right now. The best I can do is to allow her the dignity of her process and let her go where she needs to go.

I send her light as my eyes close and I am pulled again within. This time my trajectory is downward, somewhere dark, cavernous, dreadful, cold, and damp. My body shivers. I draw my silk around my shoulders. Still I descend, watching a spiraling parade of my life starting now and spinning into a vortex of time: images of *la vie quotidienne*, snippets of conversation, things left unsaid, missed opportunities, misunderstandings, misfires, things left undone, things stressed over and worried about – bills, taxes, work, obligations, everything I have to catch up, everything I'll never get done, and this nagging medical term, "diagnosis."

There's a lot of noise in here, like someone left the TV on: talking heads, an endless assault of really bad news. Smart phones, text messages, social media, freeways, gridlock.

There's a sensation of being swallowed up by the Earth, shifting hues from purple to gold to green to red; a pulsing low-cycle hum, as the images get darker and more intense. Scenes of pain, sadness, regret, and loss: things once precious now forgotten; people I've loved and lost; broken hearts I couldn't fix; all the ways I've judged and condemned myself; all the lies – the ones I've told and the ones I've believed; hidden resentments, cut corners, sellouts. All the ways I've hurt myself or been hurt, all the ways I've hurt others; the pain I carry for myself, the pain I take on for others.

I'm being pulled over the edge, into the pit of karma, past lives, collective consciousness, reptilian survival, violence, mayhem, war, starvation, suffering, inhumanity; those who abandoned and betrayed me, those I abandoned and betrayed; the traumas, diseases, fears of growing old, growing sick; losing myself, losing my loved ones; poverty, loneliness, isolation, being forgotten, rejected, exiled, cast out, persecuted, expelled from the Kingdom, entombed, imprisoned among ancient weapons, knives, guns, swords, clubs, chains, manacles, iron maidens, racks, devices for torture, execution, enslavement, death, destruction, misery, decay, the bodies of the dead and dying, some still reaching out, calling out, pleading for help and salvation… and there is nothing I can do for them.

I know I have a choice here. I know this place, and I know that its dark waters are bottomless. I know I can choose to free myself from the vicious pull of this stinking swamp. Still, I can't keep from slipping deeper, losing my grip on the muddy bank, here among the ruins, among the tangled roots and iguanas and snakes and crocodiles.

"My God," I hear myself cry out, "how can I save anyone if I can't save myself?!"

My eyes shutter open, startled by my voice. A bunch of people are like – looking at me.

I start to crack up. I try to hold it in, but it's funny as a fart in church. Save someone? Save yourself? Get over yourself, you pretentious asshole! The laughter rolls out on its own, sweeping the circle into a round of cathartic release. Maybe not a moment too soon. I might not be the only one taking himself a little seriously. Okay, deep breath.

As if on cue, Valerie quietly announces it's time for the second pour.

I line up early, do another moderate working dose, and set about changing purge buckets, laying out clean paper towels, checking in with various members of the group, offering support and counsel as needed. People come and go for a time, taking care of themselves, taking care of each other.

I'm always amazed when I see people who appear to have been experiencing the most profound challenges line up for the second pour. Candice is among them. She looks fine, lit up in fact, radiant, beatific. Her presence moves me, melts me. Generally, men and women don't touch during ceremony, but we somehow find ourselves in each other's arms in the center of the circle, a moment that has special meaning for both of us and touches with love those who witness it.

Some gentle toning on a singing bowl calls the circle back together. Adam's monochord harmonizes. Another *icaro* unifies. With a nod from Valerie, I move to open the healing mat. I clear the remaining objects and instruments, lovingly brush down the mat with a palm fan, burn a little *palo santo*, sit cross-legged on a *zafu* beside the mat.

I am joined by a few other healers, bringing sound bowls, tuning forks, crystals, light pens, hands, and hearts. Adam channels a river of sacred sound as we sit in silent meditation, sending light. It seems like a long time before anyone comes to the mat, but then they come, one after the other, opening themselves to receive. They seem impossibly many, geometrically more than the 21 we started with. There's more at the door, there's more at the door. . . The second dose kicks in like a turbine, and I am transported all at once into the Radiance.

My entire visual field is illuminated by the most stunning, shimmering spectral light, a grid of moving color, "rainbow snakes" interweaving, intertwining through all the levels of my being. I feel doors large and small opening within me, every cell, every fiber energized, clarified, electrified, vibrating. Around me, the sounds of our sacred mission intensify – the music, the chanting, the toning, the purging, the prayers.

I'm in Her temple now – moving through impossible, glittering, crystalline architecture. I hear the most soothing, celestial harmonics. I see Her, the Divine Mother, on her throne at the center of the great cosmic hall, her many arms wide and welcoming, her smile sensual, mysterious, captivating, at once drawing me in and moving toward me, her glorious temple opening up, spinning past, morphing through countless fantastic expressions, closer and closer, until at last we are together, becoming each other, merging into One.

I am completely consumed by Love, free of all that does not serve, a dance partner in perfect step with divine rhythm, flowing in confluence with my fellow healers – touching heads, hearts, hands, feet, experiencing the power and courage of each person's surrender. There's a natural rhythm and flow to our work together as healers, moving in, moving out, bringing divine masculine and feminine together, each practitioner bringing their special gifts – music, sound, light, touch, energy, Spirit.

I'm totally in the zone, operating without filters, fully embraced by the Light, fully in touch with my purpose as an instrument of healing, fully immersed in the magic and majesty of this healing moment, so powerful, so present, so alive. My crown chakra is wide open to the column of light. It fills me completely with its life-giving pulse, exploding into its rainbow components in my heart, radiating out through my hands in a bright circle.

My touch, my breath, my heartbeat, my body movements, my thoughts, my inner world seem to merge and synchronize naturally with each person who comes to the mat. Some of the sessions are gentle and deep, some are wildly cathartic, with people releasing pain and grief and trauma and fear and opening themselves to the beauty and wonder of the divine love that brought them to this place. Here, where it's safe and loving and protected and blessed, we release lifetimes of blockages, obstacles, lies, karmic contracts, judgments, and sentences. We offer ourselves and embrace the healing power of Spirit. We free ourselves to step into the truth of ourselves, revealed. It happens here and now, on the mat, in the sacred circle, as we care for you and pray for you and watch over you.

And right about now, it's getting intense. Spirits are flying around the room like kites in a windstorm. Angry, confused entities come flying out of people on the mat, passing forcefully through whichever healer they select. We release them into the nothingness from which they came. I'm working with a woman dealing with sexual trauma and infertility, my hands poised over her second and fourth chakras. She lets out a piercing wail as something large and dark suddenly springs from within her and enters my body, traveling upward through me, causing my whole body to contract and convulse. I spin away from the mat and reach for a purge bucket, but the thing is gone. Valerie has seen it, too. She touches my shoulder, draws me back from the mat. I nod, step away, clear myself with light before I return to the mat. Someone lies down. I put my hands on his head, feeling a surge of warmth from inside.

I look down at the head in my hands. It belongs to my son, Adam. I'm flooded at once by love, respect, gratitude for this beautiful being before me. I bend forward, placing my forehead on his, third eye to third eye, allowing the radiance to completely envelop us. Our breathing becomes synchronized. Adam's body relaxes. He's going deep, surrendering.

Around us, the other healers and several of our brothers and sisters have formed a circle, Aline on Adam's left, Candice on his right, Valerie at his feet, others on their knees, standing, or sitting cross-legged, holding the light – a concentric ring of angels in white, bringing their presence, energy, love and service to the divine mission being carried out in our midst. Each one occupies a sphere of light, appearing to be lit by an outside source, but since no such apparatus exists here, it must be concluded that the light we see is coming from within. Translucent white orbs float above our heads, occasionally touching down on the person receiving healing. Their presence is calming, tranquil, transformative, totally at ease, completely at home. Our sacred musicians sing "Aloha Kea K'ua" by Nahko Bear in stellar harmony.

I have one hand on his head and one on his heart. His energy travels through me as he starts to open up. I feel what he feels – his raw, primal power, his vision, his love and trust, his pain and fear. I'm moved inside, can feel my own emotions welling up, pushing against my capacity for control. I breathe and move with my son, holding his head in my hands as he starts to release what he's been holding. I know some of that shit. I was there when it happened.

I'm still here, in the sacred circle, cradling my son as he surrenders to the God within and lets go, surrounded by love, pure and unconditional. I'm overwhelmed by his courage, by how deeply he does his work, by his samurai intention to forge through the forest of his own fears into the light of his brilliance and truth. I have always held him with the deepest love and highest respect. He is, quite simply, one of my favorite human beings – never more than now. He is the very definition of a spiritual warrior. It is a privilege beyond compare to share in this sublime moment with him.

His body arches upward as if yanked up on a wire. He shudders, gasping for breath. Whatever's got him isn't going down without a fight. I get my hands under his neck and back, protecting his body as he goes through his ordeal. Aline sits beside him, stroking him gently, whispered prayers on her lips, pure angelic presence.

Candice's body seems to lift upward, rising to a standing position. Her arms open wide to include everything that's happening in her view. Her eyelids flutter in empathic ecstasy as her body writhes, undulates, surfs the waves of energy pouring out of Adam on the mat. She's Mother Ayahuasca, Kali, and Quan Yin all wrapped up in one glorious Earth woman. If there was a dragon in the room, she'd be riding it. Her left hand reaches overhead, her outstretched palm connecting with a fine shaft of moonlight streaming in through a vent in the dome that lights up her hand like a spotlight. There's a swirling vortex of energy around her. She seems electrified, like she's catching lightning. She opens her right hand and channels the energy she's receiving through her heart, to her hand, to Adam and the healers around the mat.

There's a palpable shift in the light. A warm golden glow embraces us. The orbs are attracted. They circle in close. Someone is praying an ancient language. It is clearly audible, but it is none of us, a litany emanating from the interior of our sound offering.

At precisely this moment, Adam's body appears to rise from the mat. His shoulders and feet remain grounded, with healers holding his outstretched hands, but his entire midsection rises, as though being lifted by an unseen force. Tears are streaming down his face and mine. All at once a fearsome sound comes tearing out of him, part warrior cry, part jungle roar, part rebel yell. Whatever's lifting him up lets go. His body falls back to the mat, limp.

His eyes roll back in his head. His breath stops. The music stops. Everything stops.

I look in his eyes. There's nobody there. We hold in the silence for a moment. I bend down, put my hand on his chest, listen for his breath. Still nothing. I'm kicking into rescue mode, ready to breathe for my son. I feel a soft chuckle in my ear. I look down again. Adam's eyes are open, clear and glittering. He has kind of a loopy grin on his face. I find myself smiling and chuckling a bit myself. Adam's laughter builds, shaking his belly, sweeping the circle into a chorus of joyful noise. We're all lit up, switched on, blissed out. Adam sits up, hugs Aline, Candice, Valerie, and me, and bows *namaste* to everyone in the circle. He is a living portrait of kindness, compassion, and peace. If his skin were blue, he'd be Krishna.

By and by, the circle comes back together. We replace the instruments and sacred objects on the healing mat. We sing the Ho'oponopono prayer – "I love you; I'm sorry; Please forgive me; Thank you." Many voices join mine as I pick up a guitar and sing "The Hallelujah Song": "… and even though it all went wrong, I'll stand before the Lord of song with nothin' on my tongue but Hallelujah…" At last we all join together in a final *icaro*, passing a candle from hand to hand, as we sing everyone's prayers, sending them up as an offering in harmony, gratitude and love.

The circle closes for tonight but, as we say, the work is never done. Some are still journeying and stay where they are. Others drift off to the house for food, quiet sharing, sleep. I find myself outside, drawn toward the fire. The clouds have come in. The air is wet, fresh, electric. There's a faint pink glow to the east. Lightning splits the sky; thunder rolls off the rocks.

My legs are shaking – my body is ravaged from the hours working around the healing mat. There's a vortex churning inside my body. I stumble and stagger toward the fire, which has been attentively guarded by our firekeepers. Their hands reach for me as my legs give out under me. They support me, help me down to my knees near the fire, then gently withdraw, allowing me the space to do my work. I feel their presence watching over me, protecting me, honoring the sanctity of this process.

I feel a violent shaking way down deep in my survival chakra, like tectonic plates shifting, grinding, opening, releasing a seismic wave of stored energy from my lower depths, roaring upward through the levels of my being, like a crystal tsunami. My perspective rockets upward, and I'm suddenly looking down on the whole scene.

I can see myself on my knees by the fire. I can see the firekeepers, guardians, and goddesses around me – brothers and sisters, angels in white, drifting dreamily between the temple, the house, and the fire. And now, there is only the fire. Its flame draws me in, beckons, entices, ignites me. I am ablaze from within with the ritual fire of purification, illumination, transmutation, transformation.

My body rocks with a massive spasm, and all at once I'm purging great waves of brown and red bile into the sand. Anything I've held down or suppressed; anything stagnant, vile, or poisonous; any fear, frustration, worry, or doubt; any perceived imperfection, lack, limitation, misalignment, or mistrust; anything holding me back; anything not mine; anything I took on at the healing mat; anything that doesn't serve – Grandmother wants it all now. She wants the dark entities and spirit attachments and hungry ghosts. I feel them draining into the Earth or soaring off into the night sky. She wants total surrender, total commitment, total faith. She wants me to know that she sees me – she knows my heart, my courage, my passion and devotion to our work. I am always blessed, always protected, always loved without boundaries or conditions, forever in the Light.

My breath returns to my body. I hang there for a moment, letting it in, letting it out. My eyes open. I'm still on my hands and knees. Brothers and sisters are gathered around the fire nearby. They're singing. I roll over onto my back. Someone covers me with a woven blanket. It's Candice, my love. She smiles at me, her eyes dancing in the flickering firelight. A light rain falls on my face. There's a distant flash of lightning, a rumble of thunder. The storm has passed. Overhead, the clouds are breaking up, and streaks of red and gold play overtures to the approaching dawn. A shooting star blazes by.

My body tingles, clear and fresh, renewed, restored. Here, on this rocky patch of sacred ground, surrounded by love and grace and impossible beauty, I am home at last. Welcomed. Recognized. Honored. Reborn. I have the courage to go on, with the deep inner assurance that the path I walk is the right one for me. I am fulfilling my mission, my assignment, my destiny as a peaceful warrior on the Road of Light. Tonight I sleep in the arms of my love as the sun comes up in the desert.

In the morning, we honor the tradition of the talking circle. Everyone contributes their experience, vision, growth, movement, learning. We take this time to integrate and assimilate the teachings of the sacred plants, to honor our ancestors, to acknowledge our healing, to thank one another, and to affirm our connection to Divine Source as we prepare to depart the temple for our world and our lives. But we take this with us. We come from a more heartfelt, loving, compassionate place. We listen. We forgive ourselves and others. We offer ourselves to the service of Spirit. We forge ahead. We ask that our works, our creations, and our lives be used for the highest good.

A'ho.

CHAPTER 17

Scan, Test, Adjust

"Faith is a passionate intuition."
— WILLIAM WORDSWORTH

The healing methods I have described work directly with *qi* circulating through the body's principal energy centers. These methods are very powerful and go deep and are nonlinear, even amorphous, by design. They alone can make a world of difference in the energetic treatment of many issues. When I work hands on, they are often the only methods I employ – Self Preparation, Client Preparation, Conscious Breathing, Chakra Clearing, Prayer, Bright Water, Light Circles, and Gratitude.

Remember that we are working hand-in-hand with Spirit. The healing does not take place as a function of a specific technique. The techniques give us a form through which we can attune and align ourselves with the boundless healing capacity of Spirit.

We move now into a more specific approach, bringing in the "power tools" of Spirit-energy healing: scanning, testing, and adjustments. This type of methodology can be found in numerous healing styles and traditions and is a core practice in Eastern medicine. These techniques are complex and demanding by nature, requiring a great deal of focus, imagination, and concentration. Developing skill with these methods calls for patience, practice, and trust. We're learning and developing our ability to follow an intuitive progression through levels of experience and being, with no limit to the possible combinations of energetic influences affecting the condition or healing opportunity.

Despite their complexity, despite my own inexperience and insecurity when I first started using them, these techniques have proven to be remarkably effective in my own healing practice. As I have grown into this work and utilized these methods more and more, I have adapted them into my own way of working and incorporated them into RAM Healing, typically in combination or synthesis with the other approaches we've discussed. The precise application is guided by the particular flow of each individual session. We get different information from different levels of different people. In this way, every session is unique. Similarly, practitioners have unique ways of identifying, interpreting, and interacting with the intuitive signals they receive, channel, and transmit. All of these variable elements create myriad complexities in how they might be expressed in a healing context.

The numbers alone were daunting at first. Of all the possible interactions between the body and the nonphysical levels of being, our task is to intuitively identify specific underlying causative mechanisms and then to affect them energetically for healing. This seemed like an overwhelming task, and there were times when I questioned my own fitness for the job. That's when Spirit reminded me of a simple but essential fact: it's not about me.

I'm here to facilitate an interaction, nothing more. The healing is Spirit's job. Spirit is the senior partner in this company, the CEO, the shot-caller, the director. What information we receive from a subject, how we process or interpret it, how we apply healing consciousness to it – all of these choices are made by Spirit. We are present as a function of Spirit's will and healing intention.

The whole session – who's there, how we got there, what work we do there and how we do it, what happens, how we grow and what we learn from the experience – all of these decisions are made by Spirit. In a very real way, our work is already done when we show up for the session and ask for Spirit's assistance. We don't expect to uncover every little detail. Each one of the specific points or issues we address during a healing session connects to other levels within the person, much as points along the acupuncture meridians on the surface of the body connect to deeper systems. It's not necessary to address everything. Ultimately, simpler is better; less is more.

Acknowledging the individuality of each client and practitioner's process, we soon discover that people are much more alike than they are different. This phenomenon is reflected in the larger patterns and similarities we encounter when we work with living beings from an energetic healing perspective. People differ in the details, but at the level of the Authentic Self – which is where these processes work, and why they work – we are all pretty much the same.

Intuitive Scanning

When we "see" a person energetically, the physical body seems to dissolve, revealing something like a column of radiant, colorful, fiberoptic light with bright chakra centers, connected to the Earth by luminous roots, to the heavens by visible currents, sending and receiving signals and emanating in all directions at once. Shifting to this visual perspective reveals areas of energetic blockage or stagnation within the system that allows us to focus on the areas of greatest need. At the center of the network of the human energy field lies the source connection and principal pathway for all communications and energetic influences: the central nervous system – the brain and spinal cord.

Much as we did earlier by connecting through the chakras, we now stand behind the client and connect with her by way of her brain and spinal cord. We visualize that our central nervous systems are one system, intertwined, inseparable. Often our breath will synch up with that of the client. At this point we begin a scan, starting at the top of the head, moving slowly down through the entire central nervous system and the principle nerve pathways emanating from there. If we are physically present with the person, we place our hands an inch or so above the client's body, starting at the top of the head, and tracing down the length of the spine. If not physically present with the person, such as by phone or by remote, the same result is achieved through visualization.

It is not necessary to have a degree in anatomy to do this (though it certainly doesn't hurt to practice using anatomy charts of the different structures and systems). Scanning is just taking a look inward. Generally, each level of the spinal cord innervates the structures that correspond to that level within the body. The first scan gives us more specific information on areas within the body that require focus.

We're operating intuitively and subjectively. The information we receive might be different from what we expected. For instance, the client has a stomach ache and we're getting an energetic blockage high in the chest. The key now is not to judge or evaluate any of the information that's coming through, even if it seems irrelevant or counterintuitive. Just make note of it and keep going. When the primary scan is complete, we've located a number of connecting points throughout the body – the portals through which we can begin to direct our healing energy.

Testing

This method derives from the basic kinesiology technique of muscle testing. When we do this work, we want to keep it as simple and focused as possible. The general premise here is that for every energetic influence, there are two possible responses: strong or weak. There might be any number of circuits or connections, but the responses are always either strong or weak. On or off.

The most common muscle testing technique is the Arm Push, where the client holds her arm out to the side and offers resistance. The practitioner pushes down on the client's arm to determine a strong or weak response within a given system. The Arm Push works well but is cumbersome to use over time and uncomfortable for the client.

A much more subtle version of the muscle test is the Chain Link. This is simply where the practitioner links the thumb and forefinger of both her hands together, and gives them a tug when performing a test of a particular circuit or system. If the links stay locked, that's a strong response. If they come apart, that's a weak response, which is a cue that the system needs an adjustment.

Though I sometimes use the Arm Push to establish polarity and the Chain Link if I need confirmation of something I've identified as a possible weakness, after much practice, I've simply learned to recognize my own internal responses. I know the difference between "strong" and "weak" within my own experience. With practice, you will learn to recognize your own intuitive signals. Once a weakness is identified, either between points of the body, between physical and nonphysical levels, or between nonphysical levels, it's time to make an adjustment.

Adjustments

As we move through the client's inner landscape, we'll be strengthening some things and weakening others. For instance, we might turn up "happiness" and turn down "depression," just to give an example. Testing is a very useful tool for intuitive awareness. Once we've identified something we want to shift, we do so by making an adjustment.

An adjustment is an act of direct application of consciousness with the intention of changing the signal strength of any energetic influence. Initially, I found it useful to make an actual gesture when I performed an adjustment, a little flick of my hand, like a blessing. That gesture evolved into a simple touch of my thumb to my forefinger, as though passing over a prayer bead. Adjustments (like testing) are almost always internal now, a quick placement of conscious awareness – a shot, a volt, a charge – for healing and the highest good.

Each one of the areas of interest we found when we did our scan – as well as each of the central nervous system levels with which those areas coincide – now represents an "entry point" for direct, focused healing work. From now on, we're going to be concentrating on the connections among different centers in the body, and among different levels of experience. It is within those connections that the weaknesses and blocks within the system are most often found.

The Levels of Experience

Each of us exists at multiple levels. For our purposes, the ones of primary interest are: Physical, Mental, Emotional, Psychological, and Spiritual. These are really the Big Five. Obviously, there are others – the Psychic, Ancestral, and Karmic, for instance – and we'll find ourselves working with those more esoteric energies as we move forward.

Now we focus on one of our principle points of interest and on the central nervous system connection that innervates it. We flood that area with consciousness and light. We want to know if this issue is local or referred. If it is referred, where's the signal coming from? Is it strictly physical? Or is it connected to another level, and if so, which one – emotional, psychological, spiritual? In this way, we open a dialogue with the issue. We begin to gather information from it, testing for strengths and weaknesses as we examine each issue, applying adjustments as needed.

I often describe this approach as "the systematic application of love."

So, strictly as an illustration, I might start with a scan that reveals a pocket of energetic stagnation below the left ribcage. I determine that the effect is referred from the area of the right kidney area. Now I have a connection. Is it physical or is it referred from another level? Testing reveals it connects to the emotional level, in this case to over-internalizing stress and excessive worrying. Further testing reveals it's connected to a person, a living male, which connects to fear, which shows up as a fear of abandonment, a fear of financial insecurity, and the fear connects to anger, and the anger connects to the spiritual level as a sense of isolation, of having been abandoned by God. This experience of having been abandoned by God is karmic, and goes back six lifetimes, at which point in history the client was forced to recant her religious beliefs in order to survive and then she was killed anyway, with a sword through the left ribcage to the right kidney.

This imagined sequence represents a common sort of progression. An examination of any of the entry points revealed in the scan should provide a revelatory wealth of information, intuition, and imagery. In this case, we had clues as to physical, emotional, psychic, spiritual, and karmic connections. As the material came forward, we didn't stop to judge it or determine its worth. We simply adjusted it. We strengthened the client for over-internalizing stress and excessive worry. We diminished a fear called "abandonment" related to a living male, and detached the anger and sense of spiritual isolation associated with it. We brought self-forgiveness to the misinterpretation of reality that we had betrayed ourselves, and we forgave those who we felt had betrayed us.

I just made that one up as an example, but it represents a fairly typical sort of intuitive sequence. Each point of interest revealed by the initial scan will have its own unique progression or profile. These methods provide a rich reference point for a substantial inquiry into the nature of a healing subject, and a detailed map for energetic intervention. Since the levels and categories all interact with one another, we can use these tools to help us pinpoint underlying causes of imbalances in the subject, and then adjust them.

I use this method frequently when I'm working over the phone. By its nature, it tends to bring up a lot more in the way of "information" than the pure energy techniques I discussed before, such as Bright Water and Light Circles. Those techniques can be done in complete silence, if desired. On the phone or by web link, talking serves as a helpful connecting device and also directs the flow of attention and consciousness during the session. The voice and the energy of the words themselves become additional tools in the healer's kit, to help facilitate the desired open, receptive, trusting state. It's also tough to get somebody to sit in total silence for an hour on the phone!

Unless someone is already familiar with how I work, I usually let them know that this particular technique brings up a lot of information or "stuff." Some of that material will resonate very strongly with the person. Some of it might connect less strongly or not at all. In any event, our intention is not to understand or explain the material, but simply to identify any energetic weaknesses that might be present – however they might be interpreted or expressed. Whatever comes forward, we simply want to use it in service of the deepest level of healing possible, for the highest good of all concerned. As long as we hold this as our intention, there's no way to make a mistake: we're partners now with Spirit in a timeless dance, and we surrender ourselves. We trust that Spirit knows where She wants us to go, and we simply go there with Her.

We might get extremely clear and accurate impressions of what we're working with, or the signals might be distant, nebulous, or vague. We might get words, language, numbers, feelings, sounds, colors, sensations, emotions, images. Some of the material might seem disconnected, confusing, contradictory. These obscuring energies are actually part of the issue being addressed. If confusion or uncertainty surfaces, we treat it as just another energetic influence. In other words: Where is it located? Is it strictly local or is it being referred from somewhere else? Is it strong or weak? Does it connect to any other level of experience?

For example: The condition of Uncertainty is located in the forebrain (or sixth chakra), where it connects to the throat (or fifth chakra), where there's a fear of speaking out associated with a trauma, violent aggression, and punishment if anyone ever found out, resulting in shyness, insecurity, tension, and stress, conditions that permeate the client's emotional and psychological composition. So we've gone from nebulous uncertainty to workable specifics by using the exact same process – by scanning, testing, and adjusting the uncertainty itself.

Once again, our mission is not to analyze, figure out, or understand the material running through our consciousness – any more than a light bulb needs to understand the current that runs through it. Our mission is simply to locate and adjust the energetic weaknesses we encounter.

We should also be conscious about what we actually articulate in the course of a session. People's minds will tend to latch onto the words. If there's a strong identification with what comes forward, the client's mind can become attached to that. If the material doesn't resonate, then the mind may react by invalidating the process and shutting down. In either situation, the information triggers the client's mind into judgment and evaluation, subverting their forward progression.

Similarly, material can arise that might be worrisome to the client, even embarrassing or incriminating. We want to treat any subjective information with great sensitivity and without judgment. We don't want the client to feel uncomfortable, unsafe, or defensive. Our intention is to disconnect and eliminate the harmful, destructive energies of the past, opening ourselves to replace them with the bright, clear, radiant consciousness of Spirit.

This is an act of courageous surrender on the parts of both subject and practitioner – a challenge to put aside our own doubt and resistance, to acknowledge and invite an energy greater than ours to come in and do its thing.

Our task is to facilitate opening the channel through which the healing occurs. Much of the "work" of a session is about creating conditions conducive to healing, about guiding both client and practitioner into the open, relaxed, receptive state allowing healing to occur.

Each one of the levels of experience has a variety of potential expressions and manifestations. These references are used interactively, to help facilitate the flow between the various connections.

Spirit Connections

This method tests and adjusts our "external" and "internal" spiritual connections and the pathways of communication between them:

- God
- Divine Spirit ("Spirit")
- Collective Soul
- Individual Soul
- Mind
- Brain
- Central Nervous System
- Physical Body

Essentially, we test all the Spirit connections in combination or relationship with each of the other levels.

To illustrate: We might find a weakness in the relationship between the Collective Soul and Individual Soul levels, indicating a breakdown in the spiritual relationship between the client and humanity. The result for the client might be an experience of loneliness, isolation, or abandonment, and be expressed as an inability to communicate or show emotions.

Or suppose there's a weakness between the Mind and the Physical Body levels that manifests in the client as a feeling of being incapable or helpless, with self-destructive behaviors and repeated patterns of perceived failure.

If a weakness appears between the Spirit and the Collective Soul levels, the client might be affected by things like war, disaster, intolerance, prejudice, inhumanity – conditions that affect the larger human family and each of us as individuals.

Or perhaps there's an energetic block between the Spirit and Physical Body levels, meaning that we might see chronic fatigue syndrome, apathy, depression, PTSD, eating disorders, and other addictive issues, as the body literally starves for spiritual nourishment. These conditions might be held in place by any number of thoughts, judgments, fears, traumas, parental issues, childhood religious training, and so forth.

Each general weakness we identify in the Spirit Connections opens the door to a number of possible specific causes, which in turn, we scan, test, and adjust. All of these levels interact with one another, and it is useful to test every possible combination of levels.

This method alone can provide an insightful look into the causative profile underlying the condition and send energy where it's needed most, to truly "switch on" the client's spiritual energy channels, opening them to previously inaccessible potentialities.

Chakra Connections

We've already worked with circulating energy through the chakras, the primary energy centers, with some of the other techniques. We can also use the chakras as connecting points and test the connections among them, just as we did with the Spirit Connections:

- Base of the Spine (Earth)
- Reproductive Center (sex, family)
- Solar Plexus (power, vitality)
- Heart (Spirit, love)
- Throat (emotions, communication)
- Third Eye (psychic, intuitive)
- Crown (heavens)

Once again, we test all the connections and interactions. Where we find weaknesses, we scan those specific zones for whatever revelations they may provide.

As an example (and this is a very common one), we might find a weakness in the connection between the second and fifth chakras, between the sexual center and the emotional/communication center. We scan and test, and we locate a trauma of sexual abuse involving two familial males, which manifests as an inability to trust men and maintain intimacy. We just let whatever's contained in that obstruction surface. We don't stop to judge or analyze the content. We just observe it, apply healing consciousness (adjust), and move on, examining the various systems and their relationships to one another, looking for areas of weakness, blockage, stagnation, inflammation, toxicity, internal and external influences, and any other energetic pathologies present in the levels of experience.

Clearly, this is a very detailed and time-consuming approach to the work. As I stated earlier, there are powerful healing systems to which one can devote lifetimes, mastering the nuances of the interactions and meta-connections of the human energy system. To instruct in the myriad subtleties of these processes is far beyond the scope of this chapter. We can study for years and still be beginners. But it's okay to be a beginner with this stuff. In fact, it's desirable to maintain a "beginner's mind," regardless of how much we do this work.

The more experience I get with these practices, the more I realize how much I have to learn.

Ideally, the energy of these sessions is easy, unforced, natural. When in doubt, I prefer to err on the side of simplicity. If I'm doing a scan to identify or pinpoint something within a particular system or connection, and I reach a point where I'm stumped or struggling to move forward, then I'll take a moment to simply clear the area by bringing in the Light or doing a little Bright Water, right there where my attention is focused. When this is done, I'll look at the system again and see if there's any new information. If so, I proceed with testing and adjusting; if not, I move on. I try not to let the endless complexities of the system or the fits and starts of my own learning curve hinder me.

When I first tuned in to this type of associative approach, I thought it was utterly brilliant: a systematic approach to the intuitive application of healing consciousness, derived from millennia of sacred science. It resonated with me on so many levels. I worked very, very hard at first at the mental level, trying to learn as much as I could about all the systems and their interactions, trying to "go deep," to get as detailed as possible. Over time, I realized I could work smarter, not harder, and my approach began to simplify. My style evolved into a synthesis of methods that allow me great freedom, flexibility, grace, and ease.

Anyone can do this work. Anyone can access these techniques and start using them right away. Yes, it takes practice to become adept, but it's not mysterious, exclusive, or even all that complicated. It's a simple, beautiful gift of our nature. The only mystery is why we don't use it more.

Physical Level

Generally, we scan the body first. In most cases, we're dealing with a specific physical complaint. Even when the symptoms are emotional or psychological, the body is the best place to start.

We scan at the physical level, top down through the brain and central nervous system (CNS). When we identify a weakness at a particular CNS level, we examine the area of the body that is innervated by the corresponding neural pathways. We determine whether the complaint is local or referred from another area or system of the body or one of the nonphysical levels.

Toxic influences are also tested. In the vast majority of instances, physical issues are referred from, or at least related to, other areas of the body and other levels of experience, and often held in place by one of two things: fear or trauma. As we explore the structures of healing opportunities, we can use these categorical guidelines in free-flowing combination with each other until the underlying source issue is revealed and corrected. We simply test at each level, and make adjustments as we find a need for them.

Say, we're testing and discover a weakness at the mid-thoracic spine level T6. We scan the area for any connections to areas of the body, and find a connection to the lower right lung. We test that area and find emotional and psychological components. We identify different emotions or psychological factors that might be present and whether there are any fears, traumas, or memories associated with it.

For instance, we discover trauma and abuse associated with an ancestral male. The session reveals that the client was abused by her father, who recently lost part of a lung to cancer from smoking. We apply adjustments to strengthen her in those areas. Again, this is only an illustration of how we draw connections among the different levels and define specific targets for the application of healing corrections.

We also have the grace of being able to work with a variety of techniques. I will often use this more linear, associative approach to help frame an intuitive impression about the true nature of my client's issue, to which I can then bring light. In reality, whichever method I'm working with at any given time, I'm always working with a blend of techniques, and the healing is not necessarily in the techniques. I often say it's in the spaces between the techniques; we just use the techniques to create the spaces between them.

Though it's not necessary to begin at the physical level, it is the one that people reference most often when they are seeking treatment. Since we're looking now for connections, the primary connection to any place in the body is the central nervous system. The connection between the physical level of the issue and its corresponding CNS level is always a good place to start.

The important thing to remember is that we are testing for energetic weaknesses in the connections among each structure and different levels of the client's experience. Once a weakness is identified, it's important to determine if the weakness is local or referred. If it is referred, then from where? Is it a physical symptom linked to another part of the body, to the emotions, to the psychological, emotional, or one of the other nonphysical levels? The answers to these inquiries are derived in the same way that the initial weakness was discovered: through scanning and testing the various connections. Again, until a practitioner acquires familiarity with the different body systems and their functions and interactions, it helps to refer to specific anatomy charts to help guide the awareness and focus the attention:

1. Brain

    A. Hemispheres
        – Right: *controls left side of body, space and time, processing non-verbal information, expression of emotion*
        – Left: *controls right side of body, language production and understanding, logic*

    B. Corpus Callosum (inter-hemispheric communication)

    C. Cerebellum/Lobes
        – Frontal: *(front) reasoning, planning, higher level cognition, Emotions, skilled movement, problem solving, expressive language, sexual habits, attention, socialization*
        – Parietal: *(middle) sensory processing – pressure, touch, pain*
        – Occipital: *(back) visual processing*
        – Temporal: *(bottom) auditory processing, language, memories*

    D. Limbic System ("Emotional Brain" in Cerebrum)
        – Amygdala: *memory, emotion, fear*
        – Thalamus: *sensory-motor processing (except smell)*
        – Hypothalamus: *homeostasis, emotion, thirst, hunger, circadian rhythms, control of autonomic nervous system, pituitary*
        – Hippocampus: *learning and memory, conversion of short-term to long-term memory*
        – Cerebellum: *regulation and coordination of movement, posture, balance*
        – Brain Stem
        – Midbrain, Pons, Medulla: *autonomic vital functions, heart rate, respiration, blood pressure, level of consciousness*
        – Pituitary: *hormonal processes, physical growth and maturation, sexual maturation and sexual function*
        – Ventricles
        – Cerebrospinal Fluid

2. Spine, Central Nervous System, Peripheral Nerves

    • Cervical Spine (C1–C7)
    • Thoracic Spine (T1–T12)
    • Lumbar Spine (L1–L5)
    • Sacral/coccygeal Spine (S1–S5 fused)

- Base of the Spine
- Cerebrospinal Fluid
- Meninges
- Spinal Nerves
- Peripheral Nerves
- Intervertebral Disks
- Intervertebral Spaces

3. Cardiovascular System

- Heart
- Lungs
- Arteries/Veins/Capillaries
- Red Blood Cells
- White Blood Cells
- Platelets
- Water
- Oxygen

4. Major Organ Systems

- Heart
- Lungs
- Kidneys
- Liver
- Stomach
- Large Intestine
- Colon
- Gallbladder
- Bladder
- Spleen
- Pancreas
- Skin

5. Endocrine System – Hormones Involved in all Metabolic Processes

- Hypothalamus: *hunger, sleep/wakefulness, autonomic processes*
- Pituitary: *all glands, growth, cellular regeneration*
- Thyroid: *energy, metabolism*
- Parathyroid: *calcium absorption*
- Adrenals: *stress response, "fight or flight," cellular metabolism*

- Pancreas: *digestion, insulin, blood sugar*
- Testes/Ovaries: *mental vigor, sex drive*

6. Reproductive System – Male/Female

- Penis/Vagina
- Testes/Cervix
- Seminal Vesicles/Ovaries
- Bulbourethral Gland/Fallopian Tube
- Prostate/Uterus
- Endometrium

7. Musculoskeletal System

A. Structural Systems
   – Muscles
   – Bones
   – Tendons, Tendon Sheaths
   – Ligaments
   – Fascia
   – Soft Tissue
   – Scar Tissue
   – Adhesions
   – Hematomas

B. Functional Systems
   – Postural Alignment Front-Back/Side-Side
   – Balance
   – Flexibility
   – Muscle Tone
   – Strength
   – Endurance
   – Energy
   – Efficiency

8. Toxic Influences/Metabolic Waste

A. Environmental, Food and Water Sources, Drugs
   – Preservatives
   – Chemical Additives
   – Hormones

– Antibiotics
– Putrefaction
– Food Combinations
– Bacteria
– Mercury, Chlorine, Fluoride, Lead, Petroleum, Asbestos
– Air Pollution/Water Pollution/Smoke
– Cleansers, Household Chemicals
– Nonprescription Drugs
– Street Drugs
– Nicotine

B. Body Fluids
   – Water
   – Blood
   – Urine
   – Tears
   – Sweat
   – Mucous
   – Lymphatic Fluid
   – Cerebrospinal Fluid

C. Metabolic and Cellular Waste
   – Fecal Material
   – Parasites
   – Parasitic Waste
   – Dead Cells
   – Dead Bacteria, Viruses
   – Yeast
   – Fungi
   – CO_2
   – Ammonia
   – Fetal Debris

9. Metabolic Obstructions and Pathologies

• Blockage
• Congestion
• Stagnation
• Impaction

- Inflammation
- Viral Infection
- Bacterial Infection
- Fungal Infection
- Parasitic Infestation

10. Cellular Structures and Metabolism

- Cell/Cell Membrane
- Nucleus
- Mitochondria
- Cellular Permeability
- Nutrient/Waste Exchange
- Oxygen
- Water
- Glucose
- Adenosine Tri-Phosphate (ATP – Cellular "Fuel")

11. Lymphatic System - Immune Functions and Blood Purification

- Lymph Nodes
- Lymph Fluid
- Lymph Channels
- Lymph Ducts
- Lymph Centers
- Liver/Kidney
- Urinary Bladder
- Large Intestine
- Sweat Glands
- Salivary Glands
- Lungs

Toxins and debris are flushed out by way of the lymphatic system, and this includes any waste material that might be a byproduct of the energy healing process. From our standpoint, it is important to optimize the function of the lymphatic system energetically and to perform enhancing adjustments with water, oxygen, carbon, and glucose (and other elements as needed), directly at the cellular level.

During a healing session, we eliminate energetic debris from our client's body (and our own!) through this system. I recommend "flushing" the lymphatic system with Bright Water between each major clearing during the session. The foregoing physiological systems are by no means exhaustive, and it's easy to see how we might get lost in the details. The body can be approached anywhere from a macrocosmic to a subatomic perspective and everywhere in between. We're not looking to isolate and identify every single micro-element of a client's composition. We want to use our scanning process to identify particular pathways for energetic interventions, particularly as they connect to (or derive from) the other nonphysical centers of experience, particularly the emotional, mental, psychological, and spiritual levels.

Emotional Level

Physical issues connect to primary "negative" emotions, which are in turn connected to each other as well as mental constructs. Together, these combine to create psychological structures that further solidify the issue as a perceived reality and amplify its symptomatic expression. Prevalent among these are:

1. Primary Emotional States

- Fear
- Anger
- Hatred
- Guilt
- Sadness
- Depression
- Grief
- Jealousy
- Envy
- Doubt
- Shame
- Frustration
- Despair

These states can occur in any sequence or combination. For instance, Fear might connect with Anger, which connects to Hatred. Any combination is possible, with variable frequency and intensity. We test to discover what is true for the client. Over time, these emotions can lead to chronic states that also connect with one another in various ways:

2. Chronic Emotional States

- Stress
- Anxiety
- Tension
- Fatigue
- Inability to Rest

We test for each possible combination and perform adjustments as needed. We also test and adjust for secondary emotions, which include:

3. Secondary Emotional States

- Revenge
- Loneliness
- Humiliation
- Suspicion
- Insecurity
- Bitterness
- Exhaustion
- Boredom
- Confusion
- Hopelessness
- Faithlessness
- Unworthiness
- Feeling Trapped
- Abandonment
- Regret
- Isolation
- Judgment
- Disrespect
- Abuse
- Disillusionment
- Betrayal

Again, this is not an exhaustive list, though it covers a broad range of powerful possibilities. It is intended only to serve as a guide to your own intuitive process. You're not limited to what's on this page. If something different reveals itself, go with that. If you are surprised by where it takes you, you're probably on the right path.

As with our physical findings, our purpose is not to evaluate any of the emotional material, only to apply adjustments that support the healing and well-being of the client. Scan, test, adjust, and move on!

Mental Level

This is the level that pertains to our thoughts and mental processes – what we think, as opposed to what we feel – which are, in turn, related to our emotions, behavior, spiritual health, and way of being. This is the command center for our relationships with the people and situations in our lives, as well as with ourselves. The majority of those commands are hidden, subconscious ones. Our method takes us beneath the conscious awareness and into the engine room of the underlying mechanisms. Principal areas include:

1. Relationships

- Mother
- Father
- Brother/Sister
- Partner/Spouse
- Children
- Ancestors
- Friends
- Males/Females
- Co-Workers
- Authority Figures
- Race
- Humanity

2. Money

- Home
- Prosperity
- Security
- Success
- Work
- Satisfaction
- Taxes
- Retirement

3. Health/Fitness

- Strength
- Endurance
- Flexibility
- Youthfulness
- Overall Health
- Freedom from Pain
- Freedom from Illness
- Physical Fitness

4. Self

- Capability
- Intelligence
- Self-Esteem
- Sense of Humor
- Motivation
- Goal Orientation
- Confidence
- Optimism
- Trust
- Responsibility
- Giving/Receiving Love
- Health
- Purpose/Mission
- Independence
- Being of Service
- Patience

Psychological Level

Psychological issues are mental constructs combined with long-term emotional energy. They often take the form of so-called phobias, disorders, and defenses. While much is made of the medical management and treatment of these conditions, for our purposes we shall treat them in much the same way as we approach imbalances at other levels – by simply identifying them and making corrections.

While I have seen dramatic improvements using these methods, I must stress again that these techniques are not designed to diagnose or treat any medical condition and are not a replacement for medical care. If you are under care of a physician for any medical reason, physical, mental, emotional or otherwise, make sure your doctor is aware of your complementary energy work and any proposed changes to treatment.

1. Common Phobias

- Heights
- Flying
- Public Speaking
- The Dark
- Spiders
- Snakes
- Rejection
- Confined Spaces
- Failure
- Intimacy
- Open Spaces
- Hospitals/Doctors
- Elevators
- Dogs
- Rats/Rodents
- Driving
- Success
- Being Alone
- Needles
- Aging
- Thunder/Lightning
- Blood/Gore
- Injuries/Accidents
- Disease/Germs
- Death/Dying
- Everything

2. Social Phobias

- Crowds
- Parties
- Meetings
- Dating
- Being Watched

- Tests, Examinations
- Public Toilets

3. Psychological Disorders

- Adjustment: *excessive distress to an identifiable stressor; significant impairment in work, school, social settings*
- Anxiety: *abnormal fear, worry, anxiety*
- Dissociative: *disruption in consciousness, identity and memory*
- Eating: *obsession with weight, body image, disruptive eating patterns with negative consequences*
- Impulse Control: *stealing, setting fires, gambling*
- Medically Induced: *disorders resulting from medical conditions*
- Neurocognitive: *Alzheimer's, dementia, amnesia, delirium*
- Mood: *depression, bipolar disorder*
- Developmental: *learning disabilities, autism, ADHD*
- Obsessive-Compulsive: *perfectionism, control, recurring thoughts, repetitive behaviors, avoiding contact/germs*
- Resentment
- Worry
- Self-Guarding
- Over-Protecting
- Keeping Secrets
- Hiding
- Internalizing
- Overanalyzing
- Overgrieving
- Overresponsibility

Again, our purpose is not to diagnose or treat medical or psychiatric conditions, but to bring awareness to the possible directions energetic influences may travel and in what forms they may manifest. Once illuminated, we can then bring light and consciousness to these affected systems rather than drugs and psychotherapy.

Let's use Depression as an example. From a clinical perspective, there are a number of major categories or classifications of depressive disorders. Ours is not a clinical perspective, so we're less interested in specific definitions and differences. We're more interested in the energetic roots of the whole package of specific experiences, thoughts, emotions, and behaviors labeled "depression."

Working from where the elements of the depression are found within the client – frequently in the connection between the heart and the mind, often involving multiple levels of experience and extending to affect family, sex, relationships, and work, like an octopus with its tentacles reaching into everything – we simply scan and test the systems we encounter, then perform adjustments to "turn down" the negative influences such as Sorrow, Grief, Sadness, and Pessimism, individually and in combination, and to "turn up" their positive counterparts, such as Celebration, Joy, Happiness, and Optimism. We might also do some enhancing adjustments for optimal brain chemical balance – of amino acids, peptides, and "amines" like dopamine, norepinephrine, epinephrine, and serotonin.

You don't need a doctorate in Neurophysiology to perform these adjustments, just a basic awareness of the systems and an intention to serve as a conduit for Spirit's healing energy. When the client's mind is in the surrendered state most conducive to receiving and accepting healing, the subconscious knows exactly what to do with the adjustment cues and exactly the ideal neurochemical balance. All we need to do is identify the system being addressed and apply consciousness.

If the client is under medical treatment for depression, we can adjust for an optimal outcome. If there is a chemical dependency issue, we can adjust to reduce the dependency (which does not mean to stop taking the medications!). If a decision to discontinue medications is reached, and I have seen that happen a number of times through this work, the process must be monitored by a doctor.

Spiritual and Psychic Levels

This level concerns the spiritual and nonphysical dimensions, influences, and interactions. There are countless such connections, and it would take a lifetime to test and clear them all. The ones listed here represent some major portals for these connections and provide a wealth of opportunities for energetic exploration and intervention.

- God
- Creative Source Energy
- Higher Spirit Energy
- Cosmos
- Soul Integration
- Interdimensional Being

- Spiritual Body
- Astral Body
- Emotional Body
- Mental Body
- Chakra Connections
- Spirit Attachments
- Entities
- Curses/Spells
- Past Lives
- Dead Influences
- Existential Separation
- Empathic Suffering
- Ancestral Influences
- Energy Absorption
- Places
- Traumatic Events
- People
- Objects

As we work with various issues throughout the different levels of experience, we'll discover that the issues, wherever they reside, are most often held in place by one or more of these powerful, interconnected inner structures:

- Fear
- Trauma
- Memory
- Karma

Our task, through our testing and adjusting protocol, is to locate and gently disconnect or diminish these influences, and thereby promote healing. This is a very detailed and powerful method of energetic treatment. It is important, though, not to let the process dominate, but to let it serve to focus and bring healing energy to the places it illuminates. We find that fears often fall into broad categories, such as:

- Life Events
- Relationships
- Health

- Money
- Spiritual

Testing the categories helps move the awareness toward the specific fears, which might include:

- Death
- Pain
- Loss
- Change
- Being Hurt
- Abandonment/Rejection
- Intimacy
- Commitment
- Abuse
- Love
- Losing Control
- Authority/Being Controlled
- Punishment
- Darkness
- Letting Go of the Past
- "Unsolvable" Problems
- Making Decisions
- "Missing Out" in Life
- Aging
- Physical Illness/Mental Illness
- Decline
- Poverty/Wealth
- Loneliness
- Damnation
- Divine Separation
- Being Forgotten/Forsaken
- Loss of Self/Soul
- The Unknown

Fears can be strong or weak, dominant or subtle. I usually test the strength of fear by applying a numerical gauge or scale to assess the power of the fear, with each unit representing its level of influence.

Once I know what I'm dealing with and how strong it is, I'll perform an adjustment to "bring down the numbers," with the intention to diminish or eliminate the power of the fear. The nature of the scale doesn't matter. You could accomplish the same thing by going from a high musical tone to a low one, or from red to green, or by any method that represents the transition from one frequency to another. It's just a method of consciously directing the flow of healing energy in the desired direction.

Traumas

Our survival instinct works to shield us from painful experiences by repressing them and burying the remnants deep within the subconscious, where they continue to exert powerful influences on our lives, affecting our thoughts, attitudes, emotions, and health. We test for the specific trauma, some of which include:

- Amputation
- Beaten
- Bitten
- Blown Up
- Buried
- Burned
- Choked
- Crashed
- Cut
- Drowned
- Electrocuted
- Executed
- Falsely Accused
- Fire
- Kidnapped
- Killed
- Medical
- Molested
- Murdered
- Natural Disaster
- Poisoned
- Raped
- Suicide

If a trauma emerges as part of an issue, we can test it for strength, just as we did with fear. We can also identify its vector or direction:

- You were traumatized
- You traumatized another (directly or indirectly).
- You absorbed another's trauma.

Traumas can pertain to any life stage or even past lives (whether you believe in them or not). They can be repetitive or singular events, force impacts, surgical or dental in nature. Again, whatever the cause, the intention for treatment is the same: to strengthen the client for the issue and diminish the influence of the issue itself

Karmas

Fears and traumas may test positive for karmic connections, meaning they are carryovers from previous lifetimes that have been operating unconsciously in the person's experience. By bringing the pattern into consciousness and flooding it with light and healing intention, it is possible to effect the clearing of karmas that have been present for a very long time. When karmic issues surface into awareness during a session, it is worthwhile to examine them and see what intuitive information and imagery might be associated with them – as key receptor points for healing light. I often get a detailed visual impression of an underlying karma. Often these karmas will revolve around conditions such as:

- Debt
- Another's Debt
- Payback
- Revenge
- Punishment
- Guilt
- Violence
- Suffering
- Sin
- Treachery

Memories

Beginning at the issue's connection to the central nervous system, we can pinpoint the location of traumatic memories and adjust to release, forgive, and forget them. Memories may be present in the body as sense memories (aches and pains, sensitivity, pressure, numbness, and so on), mental memories (thinking about it, talking about it, worrying about it, getting treated for it), or in any of the other nonphysical levels or energy fields. We treat in exactly the same manner as for fears and traumas – by bringing them into conscious awareness, processing, forgiving, releasing, and eliminating them.

The initial issue has now been processed and treated energetically on a variety of levels. At last, we test to confirm that the issue is complete and clear. If the subject tests strong, our work here is done.

Optimizing Adjustments

This involves energetically balancing the system for essential nutrients, elements, and frequencies. Use this protocol before, during, and after the session, as needed.

- Water
- Oxygen
- Carbon
- Hormones
- Amino Acids
- Vitamins / Minerals
- Alkaline Ph (+) / Acid Ph (-)
- Negative Ions (-) / Positive Ions (+)
- Cellular Permeability
- Water/Nutrient – Waste Exchange
- Regeneration (+) / Degeneration (-)
- Rejuvenation (+) / Aging (-)

In my own training, I have experienced different versions, interpretations, and applications of these protocols throughout a broad spectrum of healing modalities – metaphysics, Qi Gong, reiki, spiritual psychology, the martial arts – and I have explored and assimilated methods from all of these disciplines. These methods can be powerful and revealing, giving us a systematic approach to follow until all the issues revealed by the session have been addressed. They are also extremely specific and can be quite time consuming and mentally rigorous.

As my own practice has evolved over time, I find I prefer a less-is-more approach. I'll use the Scan, Test, and Correct method to reveal specific areas and levels of blockage or weakness, then go to work on those areas with prayer, light, Bright Water, Light Circles, and other elemental energies (e.g. Earth, Water, Air, Wood, Fire, Metal). The ebb and flow between modalities provides for individual variations among sessions and keeps the channels open for intuition, illumination, and inspiration.

Distance and Remote Protocols

The exact same methods apply equally, whether you are in the same room with someone or thousands of miles apart. The general observation is that Spirit light energy most closely conforms to the principles of quantum physics and is therefore unaffected by time or distance. The only requirement for working with someone is that we know they exist somewhere.

I find it's helpful for me to project myself as conscientiously as I can into the energetic field of the other person. If I know where they are, I usually sit facing that direction and have them sit, if possible, with their back to me. I know this is unnecessary since, if there's no time or distance, there's no linear direction either. I just use these little cues to orient my consciousness to the other person.

As we call in the light and begin the session, I project myself to the other person or bring them into my presence while we go through the process of connecting through our energy centers. Soon, I am holding the other person as well, both of us connected to the column of light descending from Heaven. This is the essence of working with a person by remote – to energetically bridge the distance so that there is none, then conduct the healing exactly as though the person is right there.

The same basic approach can be taken whether working at a distance, by remote (where the subject is unaware of the work being done), or by way of a surrogate – usually someone who knows the subject well or can represent them.

Ultimately, regardless of which methods we employ during a session, the healing is, always has been, and always will be in the infinitely loving and compassionate hands of Spirit. We simply ask to be used in service of this healing for the highest good, and we are rewarded with opportunities to celebrate and share in this miracle of our divine birthright.

It is far and away the most joyful, powerful, sacred, deep, satisfying, rewarding, mystical, beautiful, moving, and marvelous experience I can imagine. To be able to interact with people in this way, on this level, is a privilege beyond words. To see it work – to see symptoms clear up, people get well, get cured, get better; to see people's pain get cleared, their lives get better, their smiles come back – I simply cannot describe how profound and touching it is. It is why I keep coming back, doing this work, learning, growing, evolving, because I've seen it work directly in my own life and in the lives of many others.

The heart and soul of my message is simple: We can all do this. We are all potential catalysts for the healing power of Spirit. It is a God-given gift that often lies undiscovered or undeveloped, but is there nonetheless, ever ready to be awakened. All we have to do is ask for it and do it, asking that our lives now be used in service of Spirit's healing, and giving all glory and gratitude back to Spirit's hands.

Epilogue

On Science and Faith

"Faith is a bird that senses the dawn
And starts to sing while it is still dark."
— ANONYMOUS

There have been numerous studies on the effects of prayer on healing. The results have tended to be widely divergent and often inconclusive – but with a widespread statistical reflection of the need for more study. Some of the most credible research on the medical side comes from mind-body master Larry Dossey, M.D., who has conducted extensive meta-analysis and assessment of research on the efficacy of prayer and light healing on late stage cancer patients, and has found an impressive, statistically significant correlation between those treated with these types of techniques and recovery rates. Conversely, another of the most prestigious and widely cited studies by proponents of spiritual healing was so deeply tainted by manipulation and lies that it was eventually disclaimed by the major university that sponsored it, and proved to be the springboard for a federal fraud conviction and prison sentence for one of its authors.

It is sadly the case that, throughout history, the siren song of spiritual or mystical healing has been the calling card of countless phonies, charlatans, con men, and snake oil salesmen. You go in with a bad back and come out with an empty wallet (and a bad back). Even if we are somehow fortunate enough to experience "the real thing," we are then swept up in a landslide of criticism, resistance, and ridicule – some of it well organized by the medical-scientific machine, and some of it fueled by the irrational fears and flames of conflicting ideologies.

For every study that suggests a research link between prayer and healing, there are countless counter-arguments, rejoinders, rebuttals, and denials from legions of well-meaning "authorities," whose principal motivation seems to be to save people from their own faith. The most vocal conflict erupts between hardcore materialist science ideologues and the aggressive fundamentalism of some religions that embrace healing though divine intercession as a central tenet. The message gets all twisted up in the conflict.

I suggest that the answer lies not at the extremes but at the intersection of science and faith. For all the heated controversy surrounding the study of the topic in the West, there is an impressive background of scientific support for the medical value of practices such as t'ai chi and Qi Gong in the East. These core practices are directly involved with the movement and channeling of energy through the body and the integration of the being at physical and nonphysical levels, providing well-documented benefits in longevity, cardiovascular function, neurological conductivity, stress reduction, analgesia, and relief from high blood pressure, insomnia, and depression. These conditions obviously represent a hugely significant and profitable slice of our medical pie. The general difference is that traditional medicine aims at symptoms, while Spirit-energy healing aims at causes.

"Cause" is a fascinating subject all by itself. In the physical universe there are no observable causes, only effects. Was it the cue ball striking the eight ball, the hand moving the cue stick, the arm moving the hand, the person moving the arm, the Earth moving the person, the orbit moving the Earth, and so on and so forth, ad infinitum? Where in the chain of effects does the cause reside? This question lies at the frontier of theoretical physics, one of our most powerful and rapidly advancing sciences, which demonstrates that everything in our universe is subtly interdependent with everything else. We're all connected to and part of something infinitely greater than ourselves. Whether we choose to see God as the Old Man in the Sky who sits in judgment of our lives and hands out sentences in eternity for our behavior here on Earth, or whether we choose to view the miracle of our existence as a function of the harmonic interactions and reverberations of infinite patterns of energy from which all organization of matter emanates, the ultimate question of cause remains elusive and unanswered.

Far be it from me to try to explain quantum mechanics, especially in the context of my little book about healing, but it is safe to say that it appears that predictable *instantaneous* interactions between matched particles occur across incalculable distances of space-time as some sort of intelligent communication – a phenomenon Einstein referred to as "spooky action at a distance," since he was busy proving that things just don't move around the Universe at faster than the speed of light. It also appears that *observation* – the interaction of a quantum system with the measurable environment – plays a key role in collapsing the inherent potential of the system into a defined physical reality. The implication here is that nothing is definite until it is observed.

One of the most notable quantum theorists of our time, David Bohm, gave us an elegant description of a holographic universe comprised of an invisible *implicate* (or enfolded) order and a manifest *explicate* (or unfolded) order, and further postulated a Source from which both are generated – a Source that very much resembles the state of pure awareness as described throughout human history by saints and sages.

Just because something is unknown doesn't mean it isn't there. The search for answers lies at the heart of both science and faith. Why is it so difficult to grasp the concept of *intelligence* as a fundamental property of the universe from which all structure and function derive? The universe is both expanding and infinite, which appear at first to be mutually exclusive concepts. Perhaps it is in the shifting of our conceptual understanding that our true nature can be revealed. Perhaps it is the recognition that we know nothing that leads to the source of all knowing.

I recognize the inherent difficulty of quantifying the phenomenon of Spirit-energy healing, and it is not my intention to join the contentious debate. I believe that, as Einstein put it, "Faith without science is blind; science without faith is lame." As I've previously shared, I have a lot of respect for mainstream medicine, particularly in the areas of diagnostics and acute crisis intervention. Arguably though, there are also a lot of ways in which our dominant medical treatment model leaves the patient deeply wanting, even when the symptoms are successfully eradicated. The toxicity and trauma of our treatment approach sometimes make the cure seem worse than the disease. And little to no attention is given to the nonphysical manifestations of the illness or injury – which are much closer to the "causes" of the condition than the actual symptoms. The symptoms are merely an external representation of the whole internal composition that includes the body, mind, emotions, and spirit.

Many of us have had the experience of feeling helpless seeing a loved one suffer, feeling that there's nothing we can do, that the best we can offer is sympathy. Spirit-energy healing suggests that there is, in fact, something we can do. We can work consciously to heal the suffering. There are many, many ways to apply loving consciousness as an instrument of healing. If we accept the fundamental validity of the central premise – that there exists a form of nonlocal energy that can be consciously applied to effect healing – then we also accept that there are countless variations through which that consciousness can be expressed. Healing is not about the form; it is about a sacred, timeless interaction between Spirit and all human beings. It is, by its very nature, something simultaneously too enormous to comprehend and abundantly available to all of us. This is where anyone who would genuinely put these practices to work must take a leap of faith.

Every experience and insight throughout this process brings with it a number of choices. How is this an opportunity for healing? How do I apply this learning? How can I use it to help others? What do I do now? In a very real way, this work has caused me to completely reorganize my life around the principles of love, compassion, integrity, and service. I've confronted the resistance of my own doubts and uncertainties. I've thought, *Hey, I'm not all that good myself; how can I possibly help anyone else?*

Still, it is obvious to me that I've been called to this work, and I've been called to share it. It has been my intention to share it in this book from an authentic, experiential place, to communicate that our abilities to heal and be healed are natural gifts of our spiritual composition. The methods and practices presented here are simple, effortless, natural, and effective.

I invite you to look within and find that place inside and ask yourself if you have a calling to this work. You will know the answer immediately. If the answer is *Yes,* if you are called to do this work, then I urge you to follow your inner knowing and simply *begin.* The sooner you do so, the sooner you'll start to see results. The biggest hurdles to succeeding with this work are our own internal considerations. Put those aside for a while. You can always have them back if you want them, but I suggest that a few healing experiences of your own will quickly count you among the converted. The Spirit Light techniques I talked about earlier – Calling in the Light, Conscious Breathing, Bright Water, and Light Circles – are all you will need to get started, combined with an intention for healing for the highest good and a heartfelt desire to serve through your connection with the Divine.

Since this journey began, I've come to believe that Spirit wanted to give me a message, so She did what She had to do to get my attention. She succeeded. At times, I have secretly wished that She could've been a little gentler about it. Now She wants me to give you a message: This is Her gentle way of telling you She wants your attention, too.

Love, Light, and Perfect Healing. ~ Namaste.

Doug Heyes, M.A.
Los Angeles, California USA

Acknowledgments

"We are not alone."

In deepest gratitude for the love, healing, guidance and teachings, I stand on the shoulders of giants:

Marianne Williamson; Dr. Larry Dossey; Jay Levin; Premier Grandmaster Don Baird; Grandmaster Maria Baird; Grandmaster Steve Pisa; Dr. Baolin Wu; Dr. James Hopkins; Dr. Anthony Antonacci; Stephen Lyons; Thomas Manning; Dr. Kam Yuen; Dr. Charles Grob; Dr. David Alexander; Dr. Eben Alexander; Dr. Eran Zaidel; Dr. Sheldon Bloch; Seymour Koblin, HHP; Pennell Rock; Werner Erhard; Jon-Roger; Dr. John Burchard; Consoeur Valerie Brightheart Gill; Paramahansa Yogananda; Sai Maa; Sai Baba; Dalai Lama; Mother Teresa; Amma; Adi Da Samraj; Eckhart Tolle; Don Miguel Ruiz; Neem Karoli Baba; Ram Dass; Dr. Timothy Leary; Ernest Holmes; Mary Baker Eddy; Dr. Patricia Masters; Dr. H. Ronald Hulnick & Dr. Mary Hulnick, University of Santa Monica; Shawn Hollahan; Mary Rogers; Lesley Wirth; Michele Scott; Alfred Jacobs; Laura Dewey; Professor George Shdanoff; Michael Brian Baker; Alesha Carlander; Darakshan Farber; Dylan James Byrne; Bob Goddard, Full Circle Farms, Ojai, CA; Prasad Paul Duffy; Reverend Millie Landis, Fraternal Spiritualist Church, San Diego, CA; Reverend Basia Christ, Temple of Light, Irvine, CA; Church of Santo Daime; União do Vegetal

Douglas Heyes; J.P. Heyes; Mark Heyes; Theresa Heyes; Darcie Heyes; Jan Heyes; Adam Douglas Heyes; Aline Thiesen Heyes; Kayla Heyes-Vincent; Suzanne O'Donnell; Dane Larsen

Roy Huggins; Stephen J. Cannell; Glen A. Larson; David Peckinpah; Rockne O'Bannon; David Kemper; Bill Nuss; Thaddeus Taylor; Ron Link; Edward Rosen; John M. Stephens; Lanier Cordell

Paul Romero; Jordan Romero; Karen Lundgren; Leigh Anne Drake; Terry McDonald; Doug Hill, Richard Roth; Richard Wilson; Scott Squire; Rick Heltebrake; Chuck Miller; Alex Soto; Eddie Mykolajczyk; Big Bear Valley National Ski Patrol; Snow Summit Ski Patrol; National Ski Patrol Service;

American Academy of Martial Arts; Academy of Kung Fu; Jenny Emblom Castro; Ed Wiley; J.C. Phillips; Don Maxwell; Steve Kaman; Macie Bowdoin; Jordan Bloch; Brittney Rentschler; Ariana Brinckerhoff; Loren Lewis; Scott Robinson, Nicholas Ryan Howard

Devra Jacobs, Dancing Word Group; Thierry Bogliolo; Gail Torr; Nicky Leach; Damian Keenan; Richard Crookes; Findhorn Press

Special thanks to Robin Offner, the eye of the storm.

With all my heart to my love, Candice Land

Thank you, Bright Water.

About the Author
Doug Heyes

Doug Heyes started out as young actor. His first TV role was at the age of three, appearing in the original "Twilight Zone" series directed by his father, Douglas Heyes. Following his successful acting career, Heyes shifted to writing and spent many years in the trenches of dramatic series television, with dozens of individual episodic credits and multiple network engagements as a creative executive and producer of primetime programming. He is also the author and producer of a critically acclaimed play *"Seven Out,"* which debuted at the Globe Playhouse in Los Angeles and garnered numerous Back-Stage and Dramalogue Awards, as well as the prestigious Robby Award for Best Actor (Perry King).

In 2000, while working as a National Ski Patroller in Southern California (where he has served for two decades and led hundreds of rescues) Heyes sustained a massive spinal cord injury from which he was initially paralyzed from the neck down, unable to move, feel, or breathe. The story of his remarkable – some would say miraculous – healing has received widespread attention since its publication in *"Chicken Soup for the Soul – A Book of Miracles: Miracle on the Mountain."* That experience, which Heyes shares in gripping detail in *The Touch*, awakened him to his own healing gifts and set the stage for his total immersion in the healing arts – a journey which took him through a lineage of masters and teachers from various traditions, and back to school, where he graduated with a Bachelor's Degree in Psychology (UCLA, 2007) and a Master's Degree in Spiritual Psychology (University of Santa Monica, 2012). Since receiving his Master's, Heyes has devoted himself to developing his private practice in Spiritual Psychology, Transformational Coaching and RAM Healing. He has also created an intensive workshop – "*Awaken Your Inner Healer*" – in which he teaches the skills presented in *The Touch*, a text which now becomes "required reading" in his workshops.

Heyes is an avid outdoorsman, skier, whitewater kayaker, martial artist and long-distance athlete. Since his astonishing recovery, Heyes has competed in numerous endurance challenges as celebrations of health and opportunities for charitable fundraising. These events have included marathons, century rides, triathlons, mountain multisport events such as the gutbusting Conquer the Bear Series (snowshoeing, lake kayaking, mountain biking, mountain triathlon and the Big Bear Lake marathon) and such classics as the MS150 Bike Tour – 150 miles in 2 days for Multiple Sclerosis – and the grueling Peak-to-Peak Pedal – 335 miles between Big Bear Lake and Mammoth Mountain, California for the United States Adaptive Recreation Center.

A seasoned Emergency Medical Technician, ski patroller and outdoor rescue instructor, Heyes also holds a Red Belt in Pyong Ahn Do Won (Peaceful Mind Way) Kung Fu and has served as a training instructor for the American Academy of Martial Arts.

Doug Heyes makes his home in the coastal mountains of California. *The Touch* is his first book.